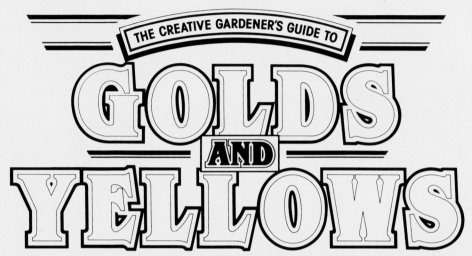

THE CREATIVE GARDENER'S GUIDE TO

GOLDS AND YELLOWS

How to mix and match over 100 stunning flowers, shrubs and trees
to create a garden of beauty

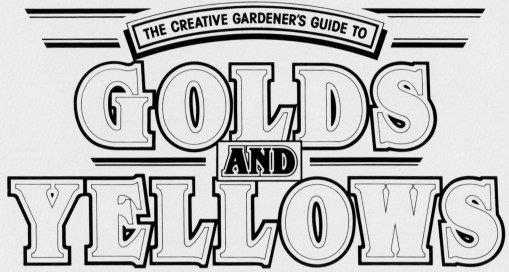

THE CREATIVE GARDENER'S GUIDE TO
GOLDS AND YELLOWS

How to mix and match over 100 stunning flowers, shrubs and trees
to create a garden of beauty

DAVID SQUIRE

a Salamander book

Published by Salamander Books Limited
LONDON • NEW YORK

A SALAMANDER BOOK

© 1986 Salamander Books Ltd.,
52 Bedford Row,
London WC1R 4LR,
United Kingdom

ISBN 0 86101 219 4

Distributed in the UK by
Hodder & Stoughton Services,
P.O. Box 6, Mill Road, Dunton Green,
Sevenoaks, Kent TN13 2XX

CREDITS

Author
David Squire brings to this series practical experience both as a gardener
and holder of many horticultural awards (including the Wisley Diploma in
Horticulture and the N.K. Gould Memorial Prize from the internationally
famous Royal Horticultural Society at Wisley, Surrey) and as the author of
14 books on gardening. He still finds time to improve and enjoy the colourful
garden at his home in West Sussex.

Editor
Jonathan Elphick

Designer
Barry Savage

Colour and monochrome reproductions
Melbourne Graphics Ltd, London, England

Filmset
Instep Print & Design Ltd, London, England

Printed in Belgium
by Proost International Book Production, Turnhout

CONTENTS

Introduction

HOW TO USE THIS BOOK

Gardeners are like painters, but with fresh canvas available to them only once a year. Borders are planned, plant and seed catalogues avidly searched and gleaned for more vibrant and longer-lasting colours, and fellow gardeners consulted. But should you or family have a predilection towards certain colours — perhaps those that contrast with established plants in your garden, blend happily against colour-washed walls, or create memories of a cherished display in a wedding bouquet — then you need further help at your elbow. You need a reliable guide which clearly portrays the range of garden plants within a particular part of the colour spectrum, and that is the purpose of this lavishly illustrated all-colour book.

The introductory pages explain the nature of light and colour and how different colours are measured and defined, according to their hue, value and intensity. There is also useful information on the influence of shiny or matt surfaces, why some colours are dominant and the effects of bright sunlight and the shadows of evening. Planning colour with the aid of a *colour-circle* is fully covered, and the concept of complementary and harmonizing colours is discussed in detail.

The main section of this *Creative Gardener's Guide* consists of five chapters, detailing pink and red plants in a wide range of garden settings: filling annual and herbaceous borders, adorning rock and naturalized gardens, bringing colour to window-boxes, hanging baskets, troughs and other containers on patios and terraces, clothing bare walls, climbing trellises or serving as a harmonious framework to knit together the various elements of your garden design. Each plant is illustrated in full colour and clearly described, including its botanical and common names, height and spread (in metric and imperial units), cultivation and propagation. Within each chapter the plants are arranged alphabetically according to their botanical names. At the base of each page there are valuable tips on using combinations of plants to create colour-contrasts, subtle harmonies, focal points and interesting shapes and patterns. Flowers suitable for home decoration are also mentioned.

At the end of the book there are two comprehensive indexes. The first lists all common names, indicating if they are used in the British Isles or United States. The second index is of botanical names, including synonyms (alternative names). The inclusion of the latter helps you identify plants botanists have recently re-classified and given new names, which are frequently sold under their old, better-known names.

This book forms part of the successful series of *Creative Gardener's Guides* and is designed to help bring further colour and interest to all gardens, whatever their size and wherever they are. Other books in this all-colour series detail the uses of *Reds and Pinks, Blues and Purples,* and *Whites and Silvers,* while further gardening dimensions are revealed in the *Scented Garden* and the *Variegated Garden.* Each book forms a comprehensive and concise guide to a particular range of colours or garden theme, but when formed into a colour library can benefit garden planning in a manner few other books have ever achieved.

Above: **Chrysanthemum frutescens 'Jamaica Primrose'**
This annual border plant creates a yellow carpet of daisy-like flowers amid a sea of finely-cut leaves.

Above: **Lonas annua**
Another reliable annual, this plant produces heads of rich golden flowers from mid to late summer. It was formerly called Lonas inodora.

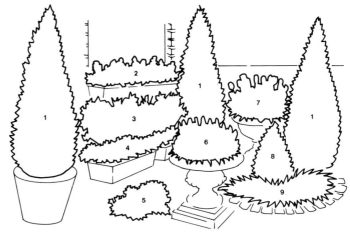

Key:
1 *Chamaecyparis lawsoniana* 'Ellwood's Gold'
2 Tulips and hyacinths
3 Daffodils
4 Polyanthus

5 *Saxifraga* 'Cloth of Gold'
6 *Muscari armeniacum*
7 Tulips, crocuses and hyacinths
8 *Chamaecyparis lawsoniana* 'Minima Aurea'
9 *Juniperus horizontalis* 'Blue Moon'

Introduction

THE SCIENCE OF COLOUR EVALUATION

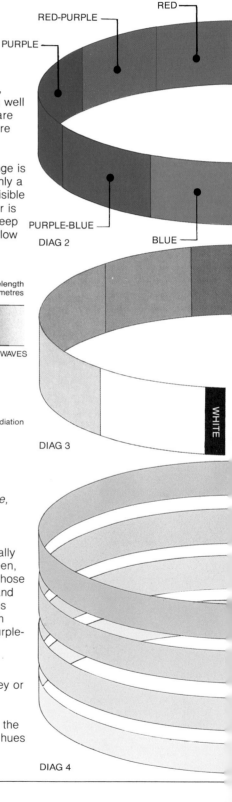

RED

RED-PURPLE

PURPLE

What are light and colour?

The vast range of colours we see in our gardens and homes, with their near infinite subtleties of quality, shades of light as well as intensity, can be accurately measured. But what exactly are light and colour? To state coldly and scientifically that they are forms of electromagnetic radiation clearly disregards their beauty, but, technically speaking, that is their nature.

Electromagnetic radiation comes from the sun, and its range is wide, from gamma rays to low-frequency radio waves. But only a very small part of this extensive spectrum is in the form of visible light, from wavelengths at around 0.0004mm when the colour is deep violet, through blue, green, yellow, orange and red to deep red, with a wavelength of 0.0007mm. The wavelengths of yellow light range from 0.000585 to 0.000575mm.
See Diagram 1, below.

PURPLE-BLUE

DIAG 2

BLUE

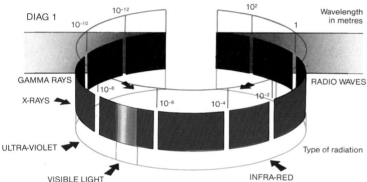

DIAG 1

10^{-10} 10^{-12} 10^{2} 1

Wavelength in metres

GAMMA RAYS

10^{-8}

X-RAYS

10^{-6} 10^{-4} 10^{-2}

RADIO WAVES

ULTRA-VIOLET

VISIBLE LIGHT

INFRA-RED

Type of radiation

DIAG 3

WHITE

Defining colour

Colours can be conceived as having three dimensions — *hue, value* and *intensity.*

Hue

This first dimension is the quality by which colours are basically distinguished one from another, such as yellow from red, green, blue or purple. For convenience, the colours so defined are those that are easily recognized, such as red, yellow, green, blue and violet. However, the Munsell System in North America defines the principal hues as red, yellow, green, blue and purple, with intermediate ones as yellow-red, green-yellow, blue-green, purple-blue and red-purple. In reality these names do no more than define points in a continuous range of hues that form a transitional and continuous band of colour. They are best conceived as a circle of pure colour, containing no white, grey or black.

If a strip of paper with ten equal divisions is marked and coloured with the five principal and five intermediate hues of the Munsell System and held in a circle the continuous range of hues and their relationship one to another can be seen.
See Diagram 2, top right.

DIAG 4

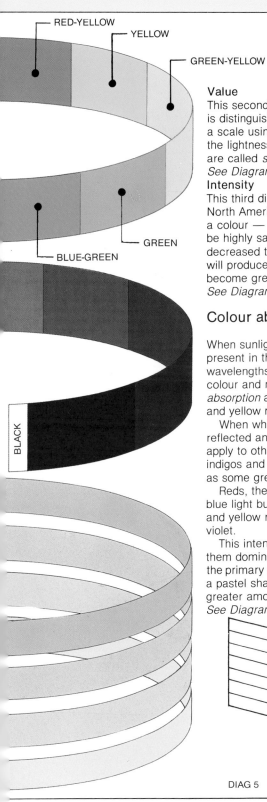

RED-YELLOW

YELLOW

GREEN-YELLOW

GREEN

BLUE-GREEN

BLACK

Value
This second dimension defines the quality by which a light colour is distinguished from a dark one. This is most easily depicted on a scale using black and white as the extremes. When defining the lightness or darkness within a colour, those with dark colours are called *shades*, while those that are light are *tints*.
See Diagram 3, centre left.

Intensity
This third dimension is also known as *saturation* or *purity*, and in North America as *chroma*. It defines the strength or weakness of a colour — its brightness or greyness. For instance, yellow can be highly saturated with colour, or the pigments slowly decreased to a point when it becomes light grey. Other colours will produce similar results, but dark hues such as red will become grey, and purple will become dark grey.
See Diagram 4, bottom left.

Colour absorption

When sunlight falls upon coloured surfaces a few of the colours present in the white light — which contains a mixture of all wavelengths of the visible spectrum — may be absorbed by the colour and not reflected. This process is known as *colour absorption* and tends to make primary hues such as red, blue and yellow more dominant.

When white light falls on a white surface, most of the rays are reflected and the subject appears white. This, however, does not apply to other surfaces. Yellow surfaces absorb the blues, indigos and violets in white light, reflecting mainly yellow as well as some green, orange and red.

Reds, the most colour saturated of all hues, absorb green and blue light but reflect red, while blue surfaces absorb red, orange and yellow rays, and scatter blue, together with green, indigo and violet.

This intensification of reds, blues and yellows tends to make them dominant. Fully saturated hues reflect no more than two of the primary colours, whereas pink, which is a desaturated red — a pastel shade — reflects all three of the primary colours but a greater amount of red.
See Diagram 5, below.

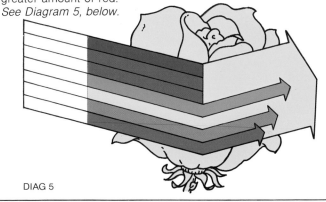

DIAG 5

Introduction

USING COLOUR IN THE GARDEN

Colour Wheels

Colour wheels are frequently used to aid colour planning in the garden. When the great English scientist Sir Isaac Newton investigated light in the late 1600s, he made a wheel formed of seven colours (red, orange, yellow, green, blue, indigo and violet). The American scientist A.H. Munsell in the second part of the 1800s researched colour assessment based on equal changes in the visual spectrum. He created a colour wheel formed of five principal colours (red, yellow, green, blue and purple, with intermediate ones between them). Other wheels have been created using four colours (red, yellow, green and blue).

However, the easiest colour circle to use is formed of three basic hues (red, yellow and blue) with three secondary ones (orange, green and violet). The secondary colours are created by overlapping the basic hues.

These colour circles indicate complementary colours (those diametrically opposite) and those that harmonize with each other (those in adjacent segments). Complementary hues are those with no common pigments, while harmonizing ones share the same pigments. Therefore, it can be seen that yellow and violet, blue and orange, red and green are complementary colours, while yellow harmonizes with green and orange, blue with green and violet, and red with orange and violet.

This colour-circle is formed by mixing coloured paints, by the process known as *subtractive colour mixing*. The other method of creating colour is by projecting three separate coloured lights (red, green and blue) onto a white surface. This process is known as *additive colour mixing*, creating colours with a different bias. *See Diagram 6, of a subtractive colour circle, below.*

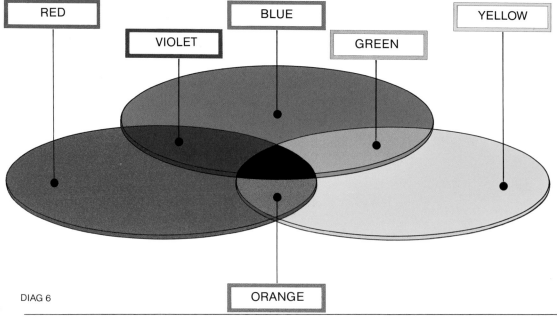

RED

VIOLET

BLUE

GREEN

YELLOW

ORANGE

Shiny and matt surfaces

The surface texture of a leaf, flower or stem influences the
reflected light and its effect on the eye. A smooth surface
reflects light at the same angle at which the light hits it. This
makes the light purer in colour than the same light reflected from
a matt surface. There, the irregularities of the surface scatter the
reflected light and create an impression of dullness. Another
effect of different surface texture is that smooth surfaces appear
darker and matt ones lighter. In Nature, however, few plant
surfaces are as smooth as glass, and the scattering of reflected
light occurs from most of them.
See Diagram 7, below.

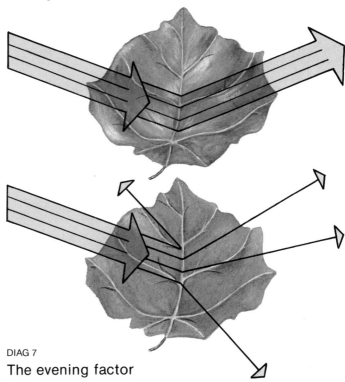

DIAG 7

The evening factor

The well-known delight of shepherds to have red sky at night,
indicating a fine tomorrow, results from a clear sky as the sun's
rays penetrate atmospheric particles and the air molecules
themselves. Even though the sky appears blue, the rays become
redder, because blue light is not created but scattered out of
white light. This change to the violet end of the spectrum makes
dark colours even darker. Golds and yellows are not so
dramatically affected as dark reds and purples and remain
relatively light in colour. Conversely, bright sunshine glaring down
at midday highlights golds and yellows (as well as whites) more
than dark colours.

Above: **Hypericum cerastoides**
*This evergreen rock garden plant
creates a dense and rounded mound,
up to 30cm (1ft) across, packed
with golden flowers, in spring.*

Introduction

HARMONIES AND CONTRASTS IN GOLDS AND YELLOWS

Golds and yellows are the brightest colours in a garden. Yellow flowers bring life and brightness, especially in spring and early summer. Yellow-foliaged deciduous shrubs and trees bring colour from spring until autumn, while evergreens give us colour the whole year round.

Large yellow-leaved trees and shrubs form ideal backcloths for dark-leaved plants. The Golden Cut-leaved Elder (*Sambucus racemosa* 'Plumosa Aurea'), Mop-head Acacia (*Robinia pseudoacacia* 'Frisia') and *Philadelphus coronarius* 'Aureus' can be used with dark-leaved plants such as *Berberis thunbergii atropurpurea, Cotinus coggygria* 'Notcutt's Variety' and *Corylus maxima* 'Purpurea' (Purple-leaf Filbert). The impact and contrasts of these plants may be too strong at close sight, so they are best reserved for planting in focal points. The yellows form the background. Position the Purple-leaf Filbert or the cotinus against a Mop-head Acacia, the berberis against a Golden Cut-leaved Elder or philadelphus. If the ratio of visible yellow to purple is about three to one, they will look balanced. Too much purple will create a gloomy sight; too much yellow will create a brash and unattractive scene.

Other yellow-flowered deciduous trees are better planted as specimens on a lawn. These include the Golden Indian Bean Tree (*Catalpa bignonioides* 'Aurea') and the spectacular *Gleditsia triacanthos* 'Sunburst', with spineless stems and bright golden-yellow foliage. They both look superb on a lawn with clear blue sky in the background, unimpeded by greys or dull, dark greens.

The ubiquitous Privet in the form of the Golden Privet (*Ligustrum ovalifolium* 'Aureum') is well worth considering for a mixed border. It bears rich golden leaves throughout the year.

Yellows and Golds of Autumn
A few of the many beautiful golden-leaved trees and shrubs have even more brilliant colours in autumn:

Acer cappadocicum
Height: 7.5-9m (25-30ft)
Five or seven-lobed dark green leaves turning butter-yellow in autumn

Acer palmatum 'Senkaki'
Height: 3-4.5m (10-15ft)
Coral-red branches and soft-yellow leaves in autumn

Carya ovata *Shagbark Hickory*
Height: 5-7.5m (15-25ft)
Leaves formed of five pointed leaflets which become rich yellow during the autumn months.

Cercidiphyllum japonicum
Height: 6-7.5m (20-25ft)
Rich green leaves turning smoky-pink and yellow in autumn

Koelreuteria paniculata
China Tree
Height: 5.4-7.5m (18-25ft)
Large leaves formed of many leaflets, yellow-tinted in autumn.

Above: **Rudbeckia 'Autumn Leaves'**
This beautiful annual creates a distinctive splash of colour (centre) in a mixed border. Its height helps to create interest.

Above: **Malus 'Golden Harvest'**
*This crab-apple bears a rich
harvest of bright yellow fruits during
autumn and into early winter,
brightening up dull days.*

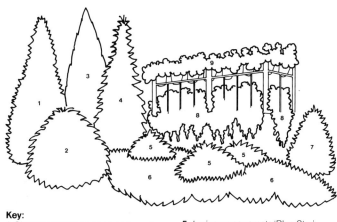

Key:
1 *Chamaecyparis lawsoniana* 'Lanei'
2 *Chamaecyparis pisifera* 'Filifera Aurea'
3 *Chamaecyparis lawsoniana*
  'Green Pillar'
4 *Chamaecyparis lawsoniana*
  'Pembury Blue'

5 *Juniperus squamata* 'Blue Star'
6 *Calluna vulgaris* 'Golden Feather'
7 *Chamaecyparis obtusa* 'Nana Lutea'
8 *Lysimachia nummularia* (trailing,
  yellow flowers) and petunias
9 Geraniums

CHAPTER ONE

THE FLOWER BORDER

Many flower gardens have been planned around specific colour themes. The great pioneer of the colour-planned garden, the English landscape gardener and painter Gertrude Jekyll (1843-1932), created many beautiful gardens on different colour themes. Her gold garden featured a number of permanent plants such as golden holly, elaeagnus, golden variegated euonymus and golden privet. Because of their year-round colour, these golden border plants are gems in any gardener's year — always reliable, colourful and of interest.

In addition to those plants with year-round colour, there are many superb gold and yellow herbaceous annual and bulbous flowers. They are ideal for quick colour, perhaps filling gaps in borders where permanent plants have yet to become established. For extra-quick colour choose annuals. Some, such as the poppy-like *Argemone mexicana* and the Pot Marigold (*Calendula officinalis*), can be sown directly where they are to flower. Tender types grown as half-hardy annuals need the warmth of a greenhouse in which to start their lives, but they have the advantage of producing near-instant colour in the garden.

For the yellow-and-gold gardener, the plate-like flower heads of achilleas, the flame-like spires of *Verbascum x hybridum* 'C.L. Adams' and the elegant frothy-headed *Thalictrum speciosissimum* are captivating.

Daffodils and tulips produce wonderful golden spring displays. Forget-me-nots and wallflowers are traditional bedfellows for gold or yellow tulips. Some species tulips are ideal for rock gardens or the front of a border. Later in the year, dahlias, like 'Claire de Lune' and 'Primrose Bryn', are naturals for the yellow and gold garden.

Left: **Summer-bedding arrangements** *can be stunningly attractive in their range of strong colours that can be blended to create harmonious schemes. Colour-contrasting arrangements have instant impact.*

THE FLOWER BORDER

apart when they are large enough to handle. In autumn, plant out the established plants in their flowering positions. In cold areas, wait until spring to do this.

Left: **Achillea filipendulina 'Coronation Gold'**
The eye-catching deep yellow saucer-like flower heads of this hardy herbaceous perennial are superb when the sun sets their bright colour alight. The flowers are excellent for floral arrangements, especially those that are dried for winter decoration.

Top right: **Alchemilla mollis**
This beautiful herbaceous plant is ideal for setting alongside a crazy-paved garden path where it helps to soften the appearance of the surface and to fuse the border with the path.

Alchemilla mollis

Lady's Mantle (UK and USA)

This hardy herbaceous perennial has beautiful light green and hairy leaves, shallowly lobed, and tiny sulphur-yellow star-shaped flowers 3mm (⅛in) wide, borne in frothy sprays from early to mid-summer.
Height: 30-45cm (1-1½ft)
Spread: 30-45cm (1-1½ft)
Cultivation: Well-drained but moisture-retentive soil in full sun or slight shade are needed. In exposed areas, this plant may require support from twiggy sticks, and in autumn cut down the whole plant to an inch or so above the level of the soil.
Propagation: Seeds can be sown in boxes of loam-based compost in early spring and placed in a cold frame. When they are large enough to handle, prick out the seedlings into boxes of compost, later setting the plants in nursery rows. In autumn, or spring in cold areas, set the plants in the garden. Large clumps can be lifted, divided and replanted in autumn or spring. However, do not lift and divide them during wet or cold weather.

Achillea filipendulina

(Achillea eupatorium)
Fern-leaf Yarrow (UK and USA)

This hardy herbaceous perennial displays 10-15cm (4-6in) wide, plate-like, lemon-yellow heads at the tops of upright, stiff stems from mid to late summer. The mid-green, deeply indented, feathery leaves are clustered up the stems. Several superb forms are available, including 'Coronation Gold', with deep yellow flowers, and 'Gold Plate', also with deep yellow flowers.
Height: 90cm-1.2m (3-4ft)

Spread: 75-90cm (2½-3ft)
Cultivation: Well-drained or even dry soil suits it, and a position in full sun. During early winter, cut back dead stems to soil level.
Propagation: Most gardeners will find it simplest to propagate yarrow by lifting and dividing the congested clumps in spring. Replant only the young parts from around the outside. Select pieces with four or five shoots.

Alternatively, seeds can be sown 6mm (¼in) deep in a prepared seedbed during late spring and early summer, thinning the seedlings to 25-30cm (10-12in)

Achillea filipendulina contrasts well with plain backgrounds and differently-shaped plants. For instance, the achillea's flowers are highlighted by a beech or yew hedge. They are also attractive when set with tall variegated grasses.

Alchemilla mollis is a useful plant which blends with many other plants, such as *Centranthus ruber* 'Albus' and roses, Red-hot Pokers (*Kniphofia*), and *Salvia haematoides*.

Right: **Argemone mexicana**
This annual is excellent for hot and dry places. Its beautiful, prickly, silvery-green leaves are able to roll up slightly to conserve moisture. The large lemon-yellow flowers appear during summer.

Argemone mexicana

Devil's Fig · Prickly Poppy (UK) Mexican Poppy (USA)

Few plants are as distinctive as this hardy annual. Its prickly silvery-green glaucous leaves are borne on sprawling stems, with the saucer-shaped flowers appearing from early summer onwards. They are lemon-yellow, scented and poppy-like, 9cm (3½ in) wide.
Height: 60cm (2ft)
Spread: 30-39cm (1-1¼ ft)
Cultivation: Well-drained, light, relatively dry soil and full sun assure success. Remove dead flower heads to encourage others to develop.
Propagation: During spring, sow seeds in the border where the plants are to flower. Thin the seedlings to 30cm (1ft) apart when they are large enough to handle. Alternatively, sow seeds in boxes of a loam-based seed compost during early spring, keeping them at 18°C (64°F). When large enough to handle, prick out the seedlings into boxes of loam-based compost and harden them off in a cold frame. Plant them in spring.

Above: *The delicate sulphur-yellow flowers of* **Alchemilla mollis** *stand above the light green hairy leaves and form a pleasing combination with the rich royal-purple flowers of* **Tradescantia 'Isla'**. *The dull green strap-like leaves of the tradescantia complete the picture.*

Argemone mexicana is best grown with other plants in an annual border. Do not let other plants crowd and hide the attractive leaves. It survives hot, dry, inhospitable places.

THE FLOWER BORDER

Right: **Calendula officinalis 'Lemon Gem'**
This hardy annual bears double yellow flowers above compact foliage during summer. It is a very reliable plant, ideal for poor soils in sunny areas. It can also be grown in tubs and window-boxes.

Calendula officinalis

Pot Marigold · English Marigold (UK)
Pot Marigold (USA)

This is one of the best known and most reliable hardy annuals, with light green, pungent, lance-shaped leaves. The daisy-like, pastel-coloured flowers in yellow or orange, up to 10cm (4in) wide, appear from early summer to autumn. There are many varieties, including 'Lemon Gem' with yellow flowers, 'Fiesta Gitana' displaying pastel colours in cream, yellow, gold and orange, 'Orange King' in deep orange, and 'Geisha Girl' with reddish-orange blooms. The dwarf types do well in containers such as tubs and window-boxes. The taller ones are best in a border.
Height: 30-60cm (1-2ft)
Spread: 30-45cm (1-1½ft)
Cultivation: Like many other annuals, Pot Marigolds grow well in poor, free-draining soils. But in a medium-rich, well-drained soil in full sun they do even better. They can even become a problem, creating masses of self-sown seedlings, but this can be dealt with by removing dead flowers. Pinching out the growing tips of young plants encourages the development of side-shoots.
Propagation: During spring, sow seeds 12mm (½in) deep where the plants are to flower. When the seedlings are large enough to handle, thin them out to 30cm (1ft) apart. To raise plants for containers, pot up seedlings in small pots before setting them in containers. If you would like to raise plants for very early spring flowering, you should sow seed in the border during late summer and early autumn.

Centaura macrocephala

Yellow Hardhead · Yellow Hardweed (UK)

A handsome, hardy herbaceous perennial with 7.5-10cm (3-4in) wide, yellow, thistle-like flower heads at the top of upright, stiff stems during mid-summer. The rough-surfaced, stiff, elongated lance-shaped leaves clasp the stems right up to the flower heads. When cut, the flowers last well in water, and bees find the flowers very attractive.
Height: 90cm-1.5m (3-5ft)
Spread: 45-75cm (1½-2½ft)
Cultivation: Light, fertile, well-drained soil and a sunny position are essential. On exposed sites, you will need to support the plants with twiggy sticks. Centaureas benefit from being lifted and divided in early spring every four years or so.
Propagation: Seeds can be sown in spring in boxes of loam-based compost and placed in a cold frame. When they are large enough to handle, prick off the seedlings into boxes of compost. When they are well grown, plant them out into a nursery bed to remain for the rest of the summer. Set the plants out in the garden in autumn. Alternatively, lift and divide established clumps in spring.

Calendula officinalis has long been grown amid old-style borders packed with annuals and border plants. It gains its common name, Pot Marigold, from being grown in earlier times in pots for use in the kitchen.

Centaurea macrocephala does well when filling bare areas between roses. The stiff stems of the centaureas allow the handsome flowers to appear between the rose blooms.

Above: **Cladanthus arabicus**
This delightful hardy annual has orange buds opening to golden-yellow, fragrant flowers in succession throughout summer. A light soil and plenty of sunshine are essential. Remove dead flower-heads to encourage the development of further blooms.

Left: **Centaurea macrocephala**
Favoured by nectar-seeking bees, the thistle-like yellow flower heads are often 7.5-10cm (3-4in) wide. They are borne on stiff stems, and are ideal as cut flowers, lasting a long time in water. The leaves form an attractive foil for the brightly-coloured flowers.

Cladanthus arabicus

(Anthemis arabica)

A bright hardy annual from Spain, with daisy-like, 5cm (2in) wide, fragrant, single flowers from early to late summer, and light green feather-like foliage.
Height: 75cm (2½ft)
Spread: 30-38cm (1-1¼ft)
Cultivation: Light, well-cultivated slightly acid soil in full sun is best. Rich soils tend to encourage a mass of foliage at the expense of flowers.
Propagation: During spring, sow seeds where the plants are to flower. Sow the seeds in drills, thinning to 30cm (1ft) apart.

Cladanthus arabicus is an ideal plant to choose for the centre or rear of an annual border, because it displays an overall mound shape. It tends to sprawl at its sides, quickly merging with neighbouring plants.

THE FLOWER BORDER

Above: **Coreopsis verticillata**
The finely-divided deep green leaves are very distinctive, and from early summer to early autumn, starry yellow flowers are borne on stiff stems. It is ideal for use in floral arrangements.

Coreopsis verticillata

An attractive busy, long-lived, hardy herbaceous perennial from the eastern United States of America, with distinctive, deep green, finely-divided leaves. The bright yellow, star-like flowers 4cm (1½in) wide, appear over a long period, from early summer to early autumn.
Height: 45-60cm (1½-2ft)
Spread: 38-45cm (1¼-1½ft)
Cultivation: Well-drained fertile soil in a sunny position suits coreopsis. Fortunately, it does not require staking in any but the most exposed sites. Cutting flowered stems back to soil-level encourages the development of further shoots. In early winter cut all stems down to soil-level.
Propagation: It is easily increased by lifting and dividing established and congested clumps in spring. Ensure each new piece has several strong healthy shoots. Do not let the roots dry out.

Above: **Dahlia 'Claire de Lune'**
This beautiful anemone-flowered dahlia grows up to 1m (3½ft), with pale sulphur-yellow flowers, shaded cream. It has strong stems, and is ideal as a cut flower.

Below: **Dahlia 'Yma Sumac'**
This is a bright decorative with double flowers. Decorative dahlias have a range of flower sizes, from 10cm (4in) in Miniatures, to 25cm (10in) or more in Giants.

Coreopsis verticillata is ideal in a mixed border, producing a long-lasting display of colour. It tends to form an abrupt, regular block of upright colour, presenting a clear outline.

New dahlia varieties are introduced every year, and many of the less good ones are abandoned. To ensure you buy up-to-date, reliable varieties send for a catalogue from one of the major dahlia growers.

Dahlias

These bright flowers can be divided into two main groups: those which can be grown as half-hardy annuals for use in bedding schemes, and those which are best in mixed borders, mingled with herbaceous plants and flowering shrubs.

BEDDING DAHLIAS

These half-hardy perennials from Mexico are grown as half-hardy annuals, displaying 5-7.5cm (2-3in) wide single, double or semi-double flowers from mid-summer to autumn. There are many varieties in a wide colour range, in mixed or self-colours.

Height: 30-53cm (1-1¾ft)

Spread: 38-45cm (1¼-2ft)

Cultivation: Bedding dahlias need well-cultivated, fertile, compost or manure-enriched soil in a sunny position. Soil too rich, however, will create excessive foliage at the expense of flowers. There is no need to stake them — unlike the large border types. Removing dead flowers helps the development of further blooms. Water the plants during dry periods.

Propagation: During late winter and early spring, sow seeds 6mm (¼in) deep in a loam-based seed compost at 16°C (61°F). When they are large enough to handle, prick off the seedlings into boxes or small pots of a loam-based compost and slowly harden them off in a cold frame. Set the plants out in the garden as soon as all risk of frost has passed.

BORDER DAHLIAS

These are half-hardy tuberous plants, easily damaged by frost, which quickly bring colour to the garden. There are several classifications and many varieties.

Anemone-flowered

(60cm-1m/2-3½ft): These have double flowers with flat outer petals and short, tubular inner ones. Flowering is from mid-summer to the frosts of autumn.

Ball-type (90cm-1.2m/3-4ft): As their name implies, these have ball-shaped flowers, with tubular, blunt-ended petals. There are *Small Ball* types with blooms 10-15cm (4-6in) wide, and *Miniature Ball* forms with flowers up to 10cm (4in) wide.

Cactus and Semi-cactus

(90cm-1.5m/3-5ft): These are divided into five groupings, *Miniature* (blooms up to 10cm/4in wide); *Small* (blooms 10-15cm/4-6in wide); *Medium* (blooms 15-20cm / 6-8in wide); *Large* (blooms 20-25cm/8-10in wide); *Giant* (blooms 25cm/10in or more wide).

Collarettes (75cm-1.2m/2½-4ft): These have blooms with a single outer ring of flat ray florets, with a ring of small florets in the centre, forming a disc.

Decoratives: These have double flowers without central discs. They are formed of broad, flat ray florets. This grouping is further divided into:

Miniature (90cm-1.2m / 3-4ft): These have flowers up to 10cm (4in) wide.

Small (1-1.2m / 3½-4ft): Flowers 10-15cm (4-6in) wide.

Medium (1-1.2m / 3½-4ft): Flowers 15-20cm (6-8in) wide.

Large (1-1.5m / 3½-5ft): Flowers 20-25cm (8-10in) wide.

Giant (1.2-1.5m / 4-5ft): Flowers 25cm (10in) or more wide.

Paeony-flowered (up to 90cm / 3ft): The flowers are formed of two or more rings of flat ray florets, with a central disc.

Pompon (90cm-1.2m / 3-4ft): The flowers very much resemble those of *Ball* types, but are more globular and are no more than 5cm (2in)

Above: **Dahlia 'Primrose Bryn'**
This semi-cactus type has beautiful flowers. All dahlias are useful for the colour they bring to the garden, right up to the frosts of autumn.

wide. The florets curl inwards for their entire length.

Single-flowered (45-75cm / 1½-2½ft): These display flowers up to 10cm (4in) wide, with a single row of petals arranged around a central disc.

Cultivation: Well-drained soil, with plenty of moisture-retentive compost or well-decomposed manure added, is required. Include a sprinkling of bonemeal before setting the tubers 10cm (4in) deep in the ground during mid to late spring. If sprouted tubers are used, take care that they are not planted too early, or frost will damage them. The young plants will need staking. Nip out the growing tips of all shoots to encourage sideshoots to develop, and if you want large flowers, remove sideshoots and buds from around the developing flowers. The removal of dead flowers helps the development of further flowers. In autumn, dig up the tubers carefully about a week after the foliage has been blackened by frost. Remove soil from the tubers and store them upside down for a few weeks to encourage them to dry out. Then place them in a frost-proof place.

Propagation: The easiest way for the home gardener to do this is to divide the tubers in spring.

Dahlias are natives of Mexico, where they grow in sandy meadows at about 1525m (5000ft) above sea-level. They were first brought to England by way of Spain, by the Marchioness of Bute in 1789.

Doronicum plantagineum

Green Leopard's Bane · Leopard's Bane (UK)
Leopard's Bane (USA)

This is one of the earliest-flowering hardy herbaceous perennials, revealing heart-shaped, bright green, shallowly-toothed leaves surmounted by single, golden-yellow, daisy-like flowers, 6.5cm (2½in) wide, during late spring and into early summer. Several superb forms are available, including 'Miss Mason' (bright yellow flowers), 'Spring Beauty' (deep yellow and double) and 'Harpur Crewe' (7.5cm/3in wide gold flowers).
Height: 45-60cm (1½-2ft)
Spread: 38-45cm (1¼-1½ft)
Cultivation: Leopard's Bane appreciates fertile, moisture-retentive, deeply-cultivated soil in full sun or light shade. In autumn cut the plants down to soil level. They may need tidying up earlier in the year if other plants are to be set close to them.
Propagation: The easiest way to increase them is by lifting and dividing congested plants during autumn or early spring. Replant young pieces from around the edges of the old clump.

Above: **Doronicums**
The cheerful yellow flowers carry on after early daffodils are over.

Above: **Doronicum plantagineum 'Miss Mason'** *The yellow, daisy-like flowers of this early-flowering herbaceous perennial are a welcome sight in spring. They are excellent as cut-flowers.*

Doronicum plantagineum 'Miss Mason' is ideal for harmonizing with spring-flowering bulbs such as tulips. These will hold their heads above the doronicums, giving added height and interest.

Eschscholzia californica

Californian Poppy (UK and USA)

This delicate, highly attractive perennial from western North America is commonly grown as a hardy annual. It has attractive, finely-cut, fern-like, blue-green leaves, and from early summer to autumn it shows saucer-shaped, bright orange-yellow flowers with silky petals, 7.5cm (3in) wide. An added attraction is the crop of blue-green seedpods, each 7.5-10cm (3-4in) long. Several varieties are available, including some lovely clear yellow and orange flowered forms.

Height: 30-38cm (1-1 ¼ ft)
Spread: 23-30cm (9-12in)
Cultivation: Light, sandy, poor soil and a sunny site are needed.
Propagation: From early spring to early summer, sow seeds 6mm (¼ in) deep where the plants are to flower. When they are large enough to handle, thin the seedlings to 15-23cm (6-9in) apart.

Below: **Eschscholzia californica**
The original Californian Poppy has been developed into a range of colours. Dry, light, poor soil and plenty of sunshine assure success. It often produces self-sown seedlings in subsequent years.

Above: **Helianthus annuus 'Sungold'**
This low-growing sunflower, with double golden-yellow flowers up to 15cm (6in) wide, grows only 60cm (2ft) high. Many other varieties grow up to 3m (10ft). Sunflowers seldom fail to capture the attention of children, and are an ideal introduction to gardening. Tall-growing varieties are excellent for creating a short-lived screen in the garden. Set the plants in groups rather than in rows for the best effect. Make sure you give them firm support in the shape of stout canes with secure ties.

Helianthus annuus

Sunflower (UK)
Common Sunflower · Mirasol (USA)

Popular in children's drawings and gardens the world over, this hardy annual from America bears gigantic, daisy-like flowers, 30cm (1ft) or more wide, singly at the tops of stems up to 3m (10ft) high. Flowering is from mid to late summer. There are many varieties, such as 'Autumn Beauty' (1.8m/6ft), with sulphur-yellow flowers stained copper-bronze, 'Sungold' (60cm/2ft), with double golden-yellow flowers up to 15cm (6in) wide, and 'Russian Giant' (2.4-3m/8-10ft), yellow-flowered.

Height: 90cm-3m (3-10ft)
Spread: 45-60cm (1 ½-2ft)
Cultivation: Well-drained soil in full sun suits the sunflower best. Remove dead flower heads and support the plants with stout canes or stakes.
Propagation: During early spring and into early summer, sow seeds 12mm (½in) deep. Thin the seedlings to 30-45cm (1-1 ½ft) apart when they are large enough to handle. Perennial sunflowers are best increased by lifting and dividing the plants during autumn or early spring, but they can also be propagated in the same manner as for the annual types.

Eschscholzia caespitosa is another species, with finely-cut blue-green leaves and yellow flowers, 2.5cm (1in) wide. A dwarf, only 13cm (5in) high, it is ideal for bare patches in a rock garden, or as a border edging.

Helianthus annuus, the sunflower, is often grown on its own in a sunny corner of a garden. But some varieties are superb at the back or centre of an annual border, mixing well with colour contrasting annuals such as *Celosia argentea plumosa*.

THE FLOWER BORDER

Left: Limonium sinuatum 'Gold Crest'
A yellow-flowered form of the Sea Lavender, with flower heads which are often dried for floral decorations during winter. Its unusually shaped foliage and bright flowers make it a superb choice for a border.

Right: Narcissus 'Rembrandt'
This is a large daffodil from **Division 1**, *with rich yellow flowers and frilled trumpets. It is superb for setting in mixed borders, or naturalizing in grass. One flower is produced on each stem. It looks best when planted in dominant clusters, rather than singly over a large area.*

Limonium sinuatum 'Gold Coast'

Sea Lavender (UK)

This hardy perennial, usually grown as a half-hardy annual, has bright yellow flowers in 10cm (4in) long clusters on erect stems from mid to late summer. It is one of the everlasting flowers, dried and used for home decoration in winter. For this purpose, cut the flower stems just before the flowers are fully open and, holding them upside down, tie them in bundles. Hang these up in a dry, airy shed until all moisture has gone. There are many other varieties, with flower colours including pink, lavender, white and dark blue, as well as various shades of yellow.

Height: 38-45cm (15-18in)
Spread: 30-38cm (12-15in)
Cultivation: Sea Lavender likes light, well-drained soil in full sun.
Propagation: Sow seeds 6mm (½in) deep during late winter and early spring, in a loam-based seed compost at 16°C (61°F). When they are large enough to handle, prick off the seedlings into boxes of loam-based compost and harden them off in a cold frame. Plant them out in the garden in late spring. Alternatively, sow seeds in spring *in situ*, but flowering is later.

Limonium sinuatum is only one of the everlasting flowers. Others include *Helichrysum bracteatum, Helipterum roseum* and *Xeranthemum annuum*, with purple flowers.

Narcissus

Daffodils (UK and USA)

Much-loved heralds of spring, these are all bright-faced flowers, with central trumpets, in various sizes. There are many different species, from 7.5-45cm (3-18in) high. In addition, there are the many garden types, again in a range of shapes and sizes, which

---

Below: **Narcissus 'Fortune'**
*A large-cupped daffodil from **Division 2**. This well-known daffodil with yellow petals and trumpets in shades from orange to red is ideal for mixed borders and naturalizing in grass. One flower is produced on each stem.*

have various classifications. Flower size ranges from 2.5-10cm (1-4in) wide, with one or several flowers on each stem, blooming from late winter to late spring.

DIVISION 1 — TRUMPET DAFFODILS (38-45cm / 15-18in): These are of garden origin and produce just one flower on each stem. The trumpet is as long or longer than the petals. They have been further divided into subsections: those with all-yellow trumpets, bicolours, white-trumpeted, and reversed bicolour trumpets.

DIVISION 2 — LARGE-CUPPED DAFFODILS (38-55cm / 15-22in): These are large-cupped, with one flower on each stem and with the trumpet more than one-third the length of the petals. These are further divided into yellow large-cupped, coloured cups, bicoloured large-cupped, bicoloured red-cupped, and white large-cupped.

DIVISION 3 — SHORT-CUPPED DAFFODILS(36-45cm / 14-18in): These have just one flower on each stem, with the cup part less than one-third of the length of the petals. Again, they are sub-divided, into coloured small-cupped, bicoloured small-cupped and white small-cupped.

DIVISION 4 — DOUBLE DAFFODILS (30-45cm / 12-18in): These have double flowers, with one or more blooms on each stem.

DIVISION 5 — TRIANDRUS DAFFODILS (up to 30cm / 12in):These are derived from *Narcissus triandrus*, distinguished by swept-back petals, and with two or three flowers on each stem.

DIVISION 6 — CYCLAMINEUS NARCISSI (20-38cm / 8-15in): These are known for their long trumpets and swept-back petals, and are subdivided into those flowers where the trumpets are more than two-thirds the petal length, and those which are less.

DIVISION 7 — JONQUILLA NARCISSI (28-43cm / 11-17in): These are of garden origin and developed from *Narcissus jonquilla*. They have two to four

---

Daffodils are universally admired. Spring has truly arrived when banks and beds glow with these beautiful flowers, many in shades of yellow. Forsythia blends well with daffodils.

Daffodils harmonize with many small-flowered and low-growing bulbs, such as the blue-flowered *Chionodoxa luciliae*. To create further interest, set these two bulbs near a blue-flowered, spring-blooming, deciduous shrub.

flowers on each stem. The flowers are highly scented and up to 5cm (2in) wide.

DIVISION 8 — TAZETTA NARCISSI (38-43cm / 15-17in):
These are descended from *Narcissus tazetta*, with its characteristic bunched appearance. They are highly scented, and divided into two main types: those resembling *N. tazetta* and those developed from crossing *N. tazetta* and *N. poeticus*. These latter ones are known as poetaz narcissi.

DIVISION 9 — POETICUS NARCISSI (35-43cm / 14-17in):
These are of garden origin and are characterized by white petals and frilled bright red cups. They are delightfully scented.

DIVISION 10 — WILD FORMS AND HYBRIDS (7.5-45cm / 3-18in):
Within this section are the species narcissi, encompassing all the wild forms, wild hybrids, and all the miniature types. Many are superb in a rock garden or naturalized in an alpine meadow.

Cultivation: They can be grown in many ways — for instance, in rock gardens, in alpine meadows, filling gaps in borders, or naturalized in woodland. The bulbs grow best in rich, well-drained soils in slight

Below: **Narcissus 'Irene Copeland'**
*A double narcissus from **Division 4**, with camellia-like yellow and white flowers. Its form is attractive and contrasts well with the trumpet types. Another good variety is 'Mary Copeland' which has orange and white flowers.*

Above: **Narcissus 'Grand Soleil d'Or'**
*A bunch-flowered narcissus from **Division 8**. It develops several flowers at the top of each flower stem, and makes a dominant display. It is slightly tender and therefore best grown in pots in the house or conservatory.*

shade. Sprinkle a general fertilizer over the soil before planting them during late summer and early autumn. Set the bulbs in holes three times their depth. (For example, it is best to set a 5cm (2in) deep bulb in a hole 15cm (6in) deep, covered with 10cm (4in) of soil.) You should set large-flowered types 10-20cm (4-8in) apart, and the smaller species types 5-7.5cm (2-3in) apart. Most daffodils should be left where they are planted for several years. If you are growing the bulbs in shrub borders, rather than in grass, plant them slightly deeper to ensure they are not damaged by hoeing during summer. After flowering, leave the foliage to die down naturally. The best-sized flowers are produced from bulbs in their second year

Narcissus poeticus 'Actaea', the Poet's Narcissus, is highly fragrant, and superb when set in large drifts in a wild garden. Bulbs are ideal for bringing splashes of colour to informal areas during spring.

after planting. However, to prevent the bulbs forming large and congested clumps in borders, lift and divide them every four years. Lift them as the foliage turns yellow. If they are left in the soil to be lifted later, mark the position, because otherwise they will be difficult to find.

Propagation: Lift and divide congested clumps after flowering, when the foliage has turned yellow.

Below: **Daffodils** *and* **forsythia** *are the epitome of spring to many gardeners. They are easy to establish and grow in a garden and seldom fail to create spring colour. Plant the daffodils in front of the forsythia in clumps rather than rows to achieve a natural effect.*

Above: **Narcissus 'Bartley'** *This highly distinctive small narcissus from* **Division 6** *has* Narcissus cyclamineus *as a parent. The petals sweep back from the trumpet. Set near the front of the border.*

Narcissus cyclamineus, with petals that curl back sharply on themselves, brings life to rock gardens and protected corners during spring. In warm and mild areas, it may appear as early as the end of winter. *N. cyclamineus* 'February Gold' mixes well with small crocuses.

Phlomis russeliana

(Phlomis viscosa)

This distinctive hardy herbaceous perennial has large, wrinkled mid-green leaves and hooded tubular flowers, each 2.5-4cm (1-1½in) long, borne in circular tiers up the stems during mid-summer. They resemble the flowers of Jerusalem Sage (*Phlomis fruticosa*).
Height: 75cm-1.2m (2½-4ft)
Spread: 75cm (2½ft)
Cultivation: Any good garden soil and an open, sunny position suit this plant.
Propagation: Seeds can be sown in a loam-based seed compost during spring and placed in a cold frame. But the easiest method of propagation is to lift and divide congested clumps in spring.

Right: **Phlomis russeliana**
The distinctive whorls of hooded yellow flowers appear in tiers up the stout stems. The attractive seedheads are useful for flower arrangements, and can be used green or dried.

Left: **Oenothera missouriensis**
This eye-catching, spreading herbaceous perennial from the Americas has bright canary-yellow flowers, 6.5-7.5cm (2½-3in) wide. These are produced during early and mid-summer.

Oenothera missouriensis

Evening Primrose (UK)
Evening Primrose · Sundrop (USA)
A superb, mat-forming, low-growing herbaceous perennial with lance-shaped mid-green leaves and bright canary-yellow flowers, 6.5-7.5cm (2½-3in) wide. It has reddish stems and blooms during early and mid-summer. The flower buds often have red spots on their undersides. Unlike many Evening Primroses, it opens its flowers during the day as well as in the evening.
Height: 13-18cm (5-7in)
Spread: 45-60cm (1½-2ft)

Cultivation: Well-drained soil is essential, because the roots tend to rot during winter in a damp, waterlogged situation. Raised beds, therefore, are often the best places, or a rock garden. During late summer or early winter, cut the plant to soil-level.
Propagation: Seeds can be sown in spring, and the containers put in a cold frame. When they are large enough to handle, set the seedlings in a nursery bed until autumn. They can then be planted into the garden. Alternatively, divide established clumps in spring. This is the best method for named varieties of many oenotheras, as they do not breed true from seed.

Above: **Phlomis fruticosa** *is the Jerusalem Sage, with whorls of yellow flowers in mid-summer.*

Oenothera missouriensis is best seen in a raised bed. This ensures good drainage and brings the beautiful flowers nearer eye-level. Its spreading nature allows it to be blended with other plants, including *Lysimachia nummularia*, Creeping Jenny.

Phlomis fruticosa, the Jerusalem Sage, is an evergreen shrubby plant, with whorls of yellow flowers, 2.5-3cm (1-1¼in) long. It blends well with the silver and greyish-leaved *Lavandula angustifolia* and *Cistus purpureus*.

Above: **Rudbeckia fulgida 'Goldsturm'**
This superb bright-coloured form has flowers up to 13cm (5in) across. 'Deamii' is another good form, with flowers 7.5-10cm (3-4in) wide, borne in abundance.

Rudbeckia fulgida

(Rudbeckia speciosa · Rudbeckia newmanii)
Coneflower (UK)

This well-known herbaceous perennial has mid-green, lance-shaped leaves and yellow to orange flowers, 6.5cm (2½in) wide, from mid to late summer. The flowers have distinctive purple-brown cones at their centres — hence the common name.
Height: 60-90cm (2-3ft)
Spread: 45-60cm (1½-2ft)
Cultivation: Coneflowers need well-drained but moisture-retentive, fertile soil in an open and sunny position. Support the plants with twiggy sticks and remove dead flower heads to encourage others. Cut the stems down to soil level during early winter.
Propagation: Seeds can be sown in spring or late summer, but for home gardeners the easiest way to increase this plant is by lifting and dividing established clumps in autumn or spring. Replant only the young parts from around the edges of the clump.

Rudbeckia fulgida blends well with the 45-60cm (1½-2ft) high herbaceous perennial *Aster amellus* 'King George', which has violet-blue flowers. *Aster x frikartii*, with wide orange-centred blue flowers, 5cm (2in) wide, is another good companion.

THE FLOWER BORDER

Right: **Rudbeckia hirta 'Marmalade'**
This is a beautiful border plant, creating a bold splash of golden-yellow, peppered with black cones. The flowers give the impression of peering upwards. They are excellent cut flowers.

Rudbeckia hirta

Black-eyed Susan · Coneflower (UK and USA)

This short-lived North American perennial is grown as a hardy annual. It has mid-green, lance-shaped leaves on bristly stems. During mid-summer and into early autumn it bears golden-yellow flowers, 7.5cm (3in) wide, with brown-purple cones at their centres. Many forms are available. 'Marmalade' has brilliant yellow flowers with black centres, and 'Rustic Dwarfs' boasts shades of chestnut, bronze and yellow.
Height: 30-90cm (1-3ft)
Spread: 30-45cm (1-1½ft)
Cultivation: These plants need a well-drained, preferably deeply-cultivated, soil in an open and sunny position. Remove dead flowers during the summer to encourage further flowers, and cut dead stems down to soil level in early winter. In exposed and windy regions tall forms will need supporting with twiggy sticks. Put these in early so that the plants can grow up and through them. If you put them in too late, the sticks will not become covered with leaves and flowers and detract from the appearance of the display.
Propagation: During late winter and early spring, sow seeds 3mm (⅛in) deep in loam-based compost kept at 16°C (61°F). When the seedlings are large enough to handle, prick them out into boxes of compost and harden them off in a cold frame. Plant them out into the garden when all risk of frost has passed. Alternatively, sow seeds 6mm (¼in) deep during spring where the plants are to flower, thinning them to 30-45cm (1-1½ft) apart.

Sanvitalia procumbens

Creeping Zinnia (UK)

This is a beautiful, low-growing hardy annual, with miniature, single, rudbeckia-like yellow flowers with black centres (2.5cm / 1in wide) during mid-summer. The form 'Flore Pleno' has double flowers. The flowers appear slightly above the pointed, oval, mid-green leaves, borne on trailing stems. Their dwarf habit makes the plants

Left: **Sanvitalia procumbens**
This hardy Mexican annual has miniature rudbeckia-like flowers during mid-summer. Like many other Mexican plants, it needs a position in full sunshine.

ideal for the edges of borders, in beds of annuals, rock gardens, and even in containers where they can trail over the side.
Height: 13-15cm (5-6in)
Spread: 15-20cm (6-8in)
Cultivation: Light but moisture-retentive soil in full sun suits sanvitalias best.
Propagation: During spring, sow seeds thinly and shallowly where the plants are to flower. When the seedlings are large enough to handle, thin them to 7.5-10cm (3-4in) apart. Seeds can also be sown in late summer in the open soil, but the seedlings need cloche protection during winter. Thin them out in spring rather than autumn. Sanvitalias can be grown to flower in hanging-baskets. In such circumstances plants will be needed for setting in the container early in the year. Sow seeds at 13° (55°F) during early spring and prick off the seedlings into pots. Harden off the plants and set them out in the container as soon as all risk of frost has passed.

Rudbeckia hirta is ideal for providing late colour in the garden, at a time when many border plants are past their best and the garden generally looks bare and colourless.

Sanvitalia procumbens is superb in the garden, but equally eye-catching as a pot plant indoors or in a greenhouse. Sow seeds in late winter or early spring in 13°C (55°F), pricking out the seedlings three to a 15cm (6in) pot.

Left: **Solidago x 'Goldenmosa'**
This superb Golden Rod, with frothy flowers in 15-23cm (6-9in) long heads during mid to late summer, gains its varietal name from mimosa, which it resembles. It is ideal in flower arrangements.

Solidago x 'Goldenmosa'

Golden Rod (UK and USA)

This well-known hardy herbaceous perennial displays tiny yellow flowers in clustered feathery plumes during mid and late summer. The narrow, lance-shaped, yellow-green leaves rise from soil level to the dazzling display of flowers. Its strong stem makes it an excellent cut plant.
Height: 75-90cm (2½-3ft)
Spread: 60-75cm (2-2½ft)
Cultivation: Any good, fertile, well-drained garden soil in full sun or slight shade is suitable. Support from twiggy sticks is necessary only in windy and exposed areas. During late autumn or early winter cut the stems down to soil level.
Propagation: During autumn or spring, lift old and congested clumps and divide them. Replant only the young parts from the outside of the clump.

Above: **Solidago 'Crown of Rays'** *is a welcome sight in summer with its cheerful golden-yellow flowers.*

Solidago x 'Goldenmosa' blends with pink and white flowers. For example, you could try the pink-eyed white *Phlox maculata* 'Omega' and the white flowers of the Obedient Plant, *Physostegia virginiana* 'Summer Snow'.

THE FLOWER BORDER

Right: **Tagetes erecta**
'Orange Jubilee'
This is a beautiful F1 African Marigold, with flowerheads proudly held above the dense foliage. It is one of the taller types, at 60cm (2ft) high. The cut flowers last well in water.

Tagetes erecta

African Marigold (UK)
African Marigold · Big Marigold
Aztec Marigold (USA)

A well-known, half-hardy, much-branched annual from Mexico. Its lemon-yellow, daisy-like flowers are about 5cm (2in) wide, and last from mid-summer to autumn. The glossy, dark green leaves, deeply and finely-divided, are strongly scented. There are many types, including single and double-flowered forms, with flower colours from yellow to orange. They also range in height from semi-dwarf (30-38cm / 1-1¼ft) to normal types (60-90cm / 2-3ft).
Cultivation: Most moderately-rich soils are suitable, and an open position in full sun.
Propagation: During late winter and early spring, sow seeds 6mm (¼in) deep in loam-based seed compost kept at 18°C (64°F). When the seedlings are large enough to handle, prick them out and harden them off slowly in a cold frame. Plant them out as soon as all risk of frost has passed.

Thalictrum speciosissimum

Dusty Meadow Rue (UK)

For distinction and elegance, few plants surpass this hardy herbaceous perennial, with its heads of frothy yellow flowers 15-23cm (6-9in) long, during mid to late summer. The blue-grey leaves are long-lasting and deeply-divided and are borne dramatically on upright, stiff stems.
Height: 1-1.5m (3½-5ft)
Spread: 60-90cm (2-3ft)
Cultivation: Thalictrum prefers a good well-cultivated fertile, moist soil and a position in full sun or light shade. In exposed areas it will require support from canes or stout twiggy sticks. In spring give a top-dressing of peat or well-decomposed compost, and in early winter cut the stems down to soil level. When staking the plants, do not leave it until late in the season as they grow quickly and may be blown over easily.
Propagation: Seeds can be sown in spring, and the container placed in a cold frame, but the easiest way to propagate is to lift and divide congested clumps in spring and replant them firmly.

Tagetes erecta can often be a difficult neighbour for other bedding plants because of its dominant size and colour, but it is useful for bringing bold colour splashes to mixed borders. You could also have a border full of these plants.

Thalictrum speciosissimum, like most yellow-flowered plants, associates well with blue flowers. Michaelmas Daisies and Delphiniums with strong blue-coloured flowers are excellent companions for it.

Trollius x cultorum

Globe Flower (UK and USA)

This is a delightful hardy herbaceous perennial, with large, globe-shaped pale yellow to orange flowers during late spring and early summer. The deeply-cleft and toothed mid-green leaves are a perfect foil for the buttercup-like flowers. Several superb varieties are available, including 'Fire Globe' (deep orange), 'Goldquelle' (golden-yellow), 'Salamander' (fiery orange), 'Canary Bird' (pale yellow) and 'Orange Princess' (orange-yellow).

Height: 60-75cm (2-2½ft)
Spread: 45-60cm (1½-2ft)
Cultivation: Rich, fertile, moisture-retentive soil and full sun or slight shade provide the best conditions. If stems are cut off at their bases after flowering, further flowers will develop.
Propagation: The easiest way for home gardeners to increase this plant is by lifting and dividing established clumps. Replant the young pieces from around the outside of the clump.

Below: **Trollius x cultorum 'Fire Globe'**
A beautiful hardy herbaceous plant for fertile, moist areas in the garden. It does well in damp areas around a garden pond. This variety flowers in spring at a height of 75cm (1½ft).

Above right: **Thalictrum speciosissimum**
This eye-catching plant is much prized by flower arrangers. Its delicate, long-lasting foliage, closely resembling that of the Maidenhair Fern, is very attractive.

Far left: **Tagetes patula 'Queen Bee'** *This yellow and red double crested French Marigold rises to about 25cm (10in) and flowers throughout summer. Its compact but well-branched growth makes it a superb choice for any flower border, where it can be used as dominant edging.*

Trollius flowers look good mixed with blue-flowered plants, but it is essential that the blue is strong enough not to be dominated by the yellow. *Iris latifolia (Iris xiphioides)* is the right blue and, like *Trollius*, likes damp soil.

THE FLOWER BORDER

Tulips

The range of these much-loved spring bulbs is extensive. They can be used to flower in spring in bedding schemes, mixed borders, rock gardens, tubs and troughs, or indoors for winter and early spring flowers. There is a wide range of species, and botanists have also classified those created by bulb experts. There are fifteen different divisions, encompassing the wide range of flower sizes, shapes and heights. These are:

DIVISION 1 — SINGLE EARLY (15-38cm / 6-15in): The single flowers appear in spring when grown out-of-doors, or during winter indoors. Each flower is 7.5-13cm (3-5in) wide and sometimes opens flat when in direct and full sun. Many yellow varieties are available, as well as white, pink, red, orange and purple.

DIVISION 2 — DOUBLE EARLY (30-38cm / 12-15in): The double flowers appear in spring when grown out-of-doors in bedding schemes, or earlier when forced indoors. Each flower is 10cm (4in) wide and rather like a double paeony. The colour range is wide, including some fine yellows.

DIVISION 3 — MENDEL (38-50cm / 15-20in): These flower later than the previous types, with rounded 10-13cm (4-5in) wide flowers on quite slender stems. Colours include white and red, as well as yellow. They look like a cross between single early types and Darwins.

DIVISION 4 — TRIUMPH (up to 50cm / 20in): These bear angular-looking 10-13cm (4-5in) wide flowers on strong stems in mid-spring. Colours include pink, red and lilac, as well as yellow.

DIVISION 5 — DARWIN HYBRIDS (60-65cm / 2-2¼ft): These are among the largest-flowered and most brilliant of all tulips, with flowers up to 18cm (7in) across during mid-spring. There are multi-coloured forms, as well as yellow, orange, red and purple varieties.

DIVISION 6 — DARWIN (60-75cm / 2-2½ft): Widely used in bedding schemes, these produce rounded flowers up to 13cm (5in) wide in late spring. Varieties are available in white, pink, red, purple and multi-colours, as well as the yellow ones.

DIVISION 7 — LILY-FLOWERED (45-60cm / 1½-2ft): These are characterized by the narrow waists of the flowers, also by the pointed petals which curl outwards, reaching 20cm (8in) during mid-spring. They look distinctive when massed in a bedding scheme. Colours include white, orange, red and multi-coloured forms, as well as yellow.

DIVISION 8 — COTTAGE (up to 90cm / 3ft): This old group has oval or rounded flowers, 10-13cm (4-5in) wide, in mid-spring. The petals sometimes have a hint of fringing, and are looser than in other forms. Flower colours include white, pink, red, lilac and green, as well as yellow.

DIVISION 9 — REMBRANDT (75cm / 2½ft): These are tulips with 'broken' colours. The rounded flowers, 13cm (5in) wide, have vivid splashes of colour on the petals during mid-spring. As well as yellow, base colours include white,

Above: **Tulip 'Golden Apeldoorn'** *These Darwin Hybrids from* **Division 5** *are superb in formal bedding displays, with flowers up to 18cm (7in) wide during mid-spring. These are borne proudly on tall stems.*

orange, red, pink, violet and brown.

DIVISION 10 — PARROT (45-60cm / 1½-2ft): These have flowers appearing in mid-spring, up to 20cm (8in) wide, easily recognizable by their feather-like and heavily-fringed petals. The colour range includes brilliant white, pink, orange, red and purple, as well as yellow.

DIVISION 11 — DOUBLE LATE (45-60cm/1½-2ft): These have very large and showy double flowers, somewhat resembling paeonies and up to 20cm (8in) wide. They remain in flower for a long period during mid-spring. Colours include white, orange, pink, red and violet, as well as yellow. Some are multi-coloured, with stripes and edgings.

DIVISION 12 — KAUFMANNIANA VARIETIES (10-25cm / 4-10in): These have been developed from *Tulipa kaufmanniana*, and have fine-pointed flowers which open nearly flat, giving the appearance of a ▶

Vividly-coloured **Darwin Tulips**, such as the dark red 'Scarlett O'Hara', combine well with white Pansies. The tulip flowers stand above the Pansies, allowing their heads to be seen through the tulip stems.

Tulips blend with a carpet planting of Daisies (*Bellis perennis*). Blue Parrot types make an eye-catching arrangement. Even two blues together — Forget-me-nots and Blue Parrot Tulips — are attractive.

Right: **Tulipa marjoletti**
This is a species, and there are more than thirty different types widely available. It grows to 60cm (2ft) and bears 5cm (2in) long blooms with pointed petals during late spring.

Below: **Tulip 'Gold Medal'**
*Large and showy double flowers from **Division 11**, these resemble paeonies and are up to 20cm (8in) wide. They remain in flower for a long period. However, in areas of high rainfall they can be weighed down by water.*

Tulips are the traditional companions of Forget-me-nots and Wallflowers. Cottage-type Tulips, with their large egg-shaped heads on stout stems, stand proudly above these underplantings.

Tulipa greigii hybrids can be mixed with Grape Hyacinths and *Alyssum saxatile* in beds with dry stone walls on one side, or in large containers. The alyssum helps to soften the container's edges.

THE FLOWER BORDER

water-lily. They open in spring on sturdy stems, and are ideal for fronts of borders, rock gardens and containers. Most have two-coloured flowers.

DIVISION 13 — FOSTERIANA VARIETIES (45cm / 1½ft): These are derived from *Tulipa fosteriana* and have large blunt-ended flowers in yellows and reds in mid-spring.

DIVISION 14 — GREIGII VARIETIES (25cm / 10in): These are mainly derived from *Tulipa greigii*, and have brilliant long-lasting yellow, red and near-white flowers. The petals reach 7.5cm (3in) long in mid-spring, when the flowers are fully open.

Cultivation: Select well-drained soil, preferably facing south and in a sheltered position. Set the bulbs 15cm (6in) deep during early winter. Space them 10-15cm (4-6in) apart. Remove dead flowers and dig up the bulbs when the leaves turn yellow. However, if the bed is needed earlier, dig up the bulbs as soon as flowering is over and heel them into a trench until the foliage has yellowed and died down.

Propagation: The easiest way is to remove the offsets clustered at the bases of the bulbs. These can be planted in a nursery bed to develop into flowering-sized bulbs.

Above: **Tulip 'Yellow Empress'** *This beautiful and distinctive* **Division 13** *tulip has long-lasting flowers of medium size in mid-spring. The flowers grow best in full sun.*

Below: **Tulip 'Giuseppe Verdi'** *These small* **Division 12** *flowers open like water-lilies in full sun. They are ideal for the front of borders as well as rock gardens and containers.*

Verbascum bombyciferum

(Verbascum 'Broussa')
Mullein (UK and USA)

This is a distinctive biennial Mullein (some are perennial) with attractive oval and pointed silvery leaves. The silvery, woolly stems are erect, and during summer their tops are clothed with sulphur-yellow, saucer-shaped flowers, 5cm (2in) wide, with pronounced stamens.

Height: 1.2-1.8m (4-6ft)
Spread: 60-75cm (2-2½ft)
Cultivation: Mulleins prefer a well-drained soil in full sun. Stake the plants in exposed areas and where the soil is rich and moist.
Propagation: Sow seeds thinly in late spring in boxes of loam-based compost, placing them in a cold frame. As soon as the seedlings are growing strongly, plant them out into a nursery bed. In autumn, set out the plants into their flowering positions.

Right: **Verbascum bombyciferum** *This is a bold architectural biennial, raising spires of sulphur-yellow, saucer-shaped flowers with prominent stamens during early to mid-summer. The silvery leaves, covered with hairs, are a further delight.*

Red Tulips set in a sea of yellow polyanthus look superb, or try an underplanting of gold *Cheiranthus x allionii* (Siberian Wallflower) and blue Forget-me-nots, with Cottage Tulips 'President Hoover' (orange-red) and 'Mrs. John T Scheepers' (yellow).

Yellow backgrounds are very striking: you could try an underplanting of a yellow Viola, with the Single Early Tulip 'Keizerskroom' (with yellow and red flowers) above it.

Further plants to consider

Asphodeline lutea

(Asphodelus luteus)
Asphodel · King's Spear · Jacob's Rod (UK)   Asphodel · King's Spear (USA)

Height: 90cm-1m (3-3½ft)   Spread: 75-90cm (2½-3ft)
An upright, stately herbaceous perennial with dark green grassy leaves and fragrant, star-like, bright yellow flowers arranged up stiff stems during mid-summer.

Buphthalmum salicifolium

Willow-leaf Ox-eye (UK)   Thoroughwax (USA)

Height: 45-60cm (1½-2ft)   Spread: 60-75cm (2-2½ft)
A hardy herbaceous perennial which spreads by underground runners. It is ideal for moist soils. During early to mid-summer it bears bright, golden-yellow, daisy-like flowers, which measure 4cm (1½in) across.

Digitalis grandiflora

(Digitalis ambigua)
Yellow Foxglove (UK and USA)

Height: 60-90cm (2-3ft)   Spread: 38-45cm (1¼-1½ft)
A perennial with pale creamy-yellow, foxglove-like flowers, 5cm (2in) long, during mid to late summer. The flowers are borne on spikes up to 60cm (2ft).

Helenium autumnale 'Golden Youth'

Height: 75cm (2½ft)   Spread: 38-45cm (1¼-1½ft)
A beautiful free-flowering, hardy herbaceous perennial with large yellow, daisy-like flowers during late summer and into autumn. There are several other good yellow-flowering forms, such as 'Butterpat' and 'Wyndley' (yellow and copper).

Heliopsis scabra

Orange Sunflower (UK)   Oxeye (USA)

A beautiful hardy herbaceous perennial, ideal for brightening up a border during mid to late summer, with large, daisy-like yellow flowers. Varieties to consider include 'Gold Plume' (rich yellow), 'Goldgreenheart' (lemon-yellow) and 'Incomparabilis' (orange-yellow).

Hunnemannia fumariifolia

Mexican Tulip Poppy (UK)   Mexican Tulip Poppy · Golden Cup (USA)

Height: 45-60cm (1½-2ft)   Spread: 38-45cm (1¼-1½ft)
A beautiful poppy-like hardy annual with finely-cut, blue-green foliage and cup-shaped yellow flowers on long stems during late summer.

Verbascum thapsus, the Great Mullein from Europe, has yellow flowers and thick woolly leaves and was called Bullock's Lungwort. It was also associated with witches and earned the name Hag-taper.

CHAPTER TWO

ROCK AND NATURALIZED GARDENS

Rock gardens usually receive more love and attention than any other garden area of equal size. The plants are diminutive, often early-flowering and frequently fussy about drainage. Though they need a certain amount of special care, yard-for-yard, rock gardens can support a greater range of plants than other sites.

Naturalized gardens — perhaps helping a garden pond fuse into the overall garden scene, on a warm grassy bank at the side of a rock garden, or sheltered and semi-shaded beneath a canopy of deciduous trees — can all feature beautiful yellow-flowered plants. With the pressing desire of many people to find their roots and return to a natural way of living, naturalized areas have become increasingly popular. However, take care not to use invasive plants which will soon dominate or suffocate choice plants.

The range of golden plants suitable for a rock garden is wide, from yellow-leaved dwarf and slow-growing conifers to bulb or corm-bearing plants such as the Winter Aconite (*Eranthis hyemalis*), the Yellow Star Flower (*Sternbergia lutea*) and *Tulipa tarda*, a beautiful species tulip. Miniature daffodils, ideal for naturalizing in short and fine grass, as well as for planting in a rock garden, should not be forgotten. Try the Hoop Petticoat Daffodil (*Narcissus bulbocodium*) or the eye-catching *Narcissus cyclamineus*.

For large rock gardens several members of the broom family are ideal: the hybrid *Cytisus x beanii*, *Genista pilosa*, *G. lydia* and *G sagittalis*. Some of these are superb when allowed to trail over large rocks or from the top of a dry stone wall.

Small herbaceous perennials also do well in rock and naturalized gardens: these include *Solidago brachystachys* and *Achillea tomentosa*.

Left: **Hypericum cerastoides,** *an evergreen, creates masses of bright yellow flowers 2.5-4cm (1-1½in) wide during late spring and early summer.*

ROCK AND NATURALIZED GARDENS

Right: **Achillea tomentosa**
This delightful herbaceous perennial has mats of fern-like leaves and tightly-packed flower head during mid to late summer. It needs well-drained soil and a sunny position.

Achillea tomentosa

This is a bright, dwarf herbaceous perennial for the rock garden, crevices between natural stone paths and in dry stone walls. It displays long, softly hairy and fern-like grey-green leaves which form prostrate mats. Densely-packed heads of bright yellow flowers, 7.5cm (3in) wide, appear on 15cm (6in) long stems during mid to late summer.

Height: 15-18cm (6-7in)
Spread: 25-30cm (10-12in)
Cultivation: Achilleas need a well-drained soil and a sunny position. Avoid damp conditions which encourage slugs to graze on the foliage.
Propagation: The easiest way to increase this plant is by division of the roots in autumn or spring. Spring is the best time, as autumn-divided plants need to be overwintered in a cold frame. Alternatively, take soft cuttings in mid-summer and place in sandy compost in pots in a cold frame.

Alyssum saxatile

Gold Dust · Golden Tuft · Rock Madwort (UK)

This well-known shrubby evergreen perennial has a tumbling and cascading growth habit, making it ideal for covering dry stone walls. Its grey-green leaves are lance-shaped, with 10-15cm (4-6in) wide heads of golden-yellow flowers in early summer. Several superb forms are widely available, including 'Dudley Neville', with biscuit-yellow flowers, and 'Citrinum', with bright lemon-yellow flowers.

Height: 23-30cm (9-12in)
Spread: 30-45cm (1-1½ft)
Cultivation: Ordinary garden soil,

Achillea tomentosa is ideal for setting between natural paving slabs or in crevices at the top of dry stone walls. In a rock garden, sprinkle stone chippings around the plant for an attractive background and good drainage.

Alyssum saxatile can be used in combination with many other plants, from the biennial Forget-me-not, polyanthus, the bulbous *Chionodoxa luciliae* and Grape Hyacinth to the rock-garden aubrietia.

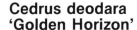

well-drained, and a position in full sun are needed. After flowering, cut the plants back to encourage the development of young growths.
Propagation: Named types do not come true from seed and are therefore best raised by taking 5-7.5cm (2-3in) long cuttings in summer. Insert them into equal parts peat and sharp sand. When the plants are rooted, pot them up into loam-based compost and replace in a cold frame. Plant out into the garden in spring. The young plants are best set out in their new positions in spring, though this can be done in late summer in mild areas.

Left: **Alyssum saxatile 'Dudley Neville'**
This beautiful shrubby perennial has biscuit-yellow flowers which cascade down walls in early summer like a coloured waterfall. Other forms are brighter.

Cedrus deodara 'Golden Horizon'

This semi-prostrate slow-growing evergreen conifer is often twice as wide as it is high. It has graceful, pendulous, golden-leaved branches, and as the dwarf tree matures, it resembles a golden cascade.
Height: 60-75cm (2-2½ft)
Spread: 75-1.2m (2½-4ft)
Cultivation: Well-drained garden soil suits it — it will do well even in coastal areas.
Propagation: It is a grafted form, so its propagation is best left to expert nurserymen.

Below: **Cedrus deodara 'Golden Horizon'**
This beautiful slow-growing evergreen conifer produces a cascading array of golden foliage. Its spread is frequently up to twice its height.

Above: **Chamaecyparis lawsoniana 'Aurea Densa'**
This dense, slow-growing dwarf conifer is ideal for rock gardens, containers and stone sinks. It can also be planted among small ericas and heathers.

Chamaecyparis lawsoniana 'Aurea Densa'

A densely-foliaged slow-growing dwarf evergreen conifer, this tree is ideal for rock gardens and containers. It has a dome-shaped habit, with bright golden-yellow foliage. After ten years, it reaches about 30-50cm (12-20in) high and 25-38cm (10-15in) wide.
Height: 90cm-1m (3-3½ft)
Spread: 75-90cm (2½-3ft)
Cultivation: Well-drained garden soil is essential for success, and a position in full sun to help maintain the golden-yellow foliage.
Propagation: Take 10cm (4in) long heel cuttings in spring, inserting them into equal parts peat and sharp sand. Place them in a cold frame, and, when rooted, pot up into small pots. Plunge them into soil in a nursery bed and plant them out into a sheltered bed in autumn for a few years.

Cedrus deodara 'Golden Horizon' is ideal in a heather garden, surrounded by prostrate colour-contrasting conifers. Alternatively, place it between blue-foliaged upright conifers, such as *Picea pungens* 'Hoopsii' or *Picea pungens* 'Koster'.

Chamaecyparis lawsoniana 'Aurea Densa' is ideal for a small collection of dwarf and slow-growing conifers, and looks attractive when positioned among prostrate blue-foliaged junipers such as *Juniperus horizontalis* 'Blue Moon'.

nursery bed. During autumn, put the young plants into a nursery bed for three or four years before setting them out in their permanent positions. It is often confused with *C.l.* 'Aurea Densa', which has a compact habit and golden-yellow foliage arranged in short, densely-packed and flattened sprays. In *C.l.* 'Minima Aurea' the sprays of foliage are mainly arranged vertically. Both, however, are ideal and distinctive conifers for a rock garden.

Left: **Chamaecyparis lawsoniana 'Minima Aurea'**
A beautifully-foliaged dwarf conifer, it also has an attractive shape. The golden-yellow foliage remains bright throughout the year, and grows in a distinctive vertical pattern.

Below: **Chamaecyparis pisifera 'Filifera Aurea'**
A slow-growing conifer, this variety is prized for its thread-like golden foliage which droops at its tips and gives a weeping appearance. Eventually, it will develop into a pretty large tree.

Chamaecyparis lawsoniana 'Minima Aurea'

An attractive, slow-growing, evergreen conifer with a rounded form and vertically-arranged, scale-like, golden-yellow leaves, it reaches 50cm (20in) high and 40cm (16in) wide. It is ideal for planting in a rock garden.
Height: 1m (3½ft)
Spread: 80cm (32in)
Cultivation: This conifer needs ordinary well-drained garden soil, and a position in the open. It does best in full sun, which helps to maintain the golden foliage.
Propagation: During spring, take 10cm (4in) long heel cuttings, inserting them into equal parts peat and sharp sand and placing them in a cold frame. When rooted, pot them up into small pots and plunge these into soil in a

Chamaecyparis lawsoniana 'Minima Aurea' looks superb on its own in a rock garden, or in a heather garden where it can be set in threes in a sea of white-flowered ericas. Set them several feet apart so that their shapes are not impaired.

Chamaecyparis pisifera 'Filifera Aurea'

This distinctive slow-growing evergreen conifer has thread-like golden foliage which trails at its tips, giving it a weeping appearance. It has a mop-head, somewhat conical shape. It is ideal for setting in a large rock garden or in a heather garden. After ten years it will reach 1m (3½ft) high, with a spread of 1.2m (4ft). Several other forms of this species are a delight in the rock garden. These include the conical *C.p.* 'Plumosa Aurea Nana' with a height of 90cm (3ft) and a 60cm (2ft) spread. It retains its golden colour throughout the year. *C.p.* 'Nana Aureovariegata' is another lovely form, with golden variegated foliage. Other golden forms include *C.p.* 'Squarrosa Sulphurea' with a rounded form and bright sulphur-yellow foliage, and *C.p.* 'Gold Spangle' with an open but rounded form and bright golden foliage. It is especially attractive in winter.
Height: 4.5m (15ft)
Spread: 4.5-5.4m (15-18ft)

Cultivation: Well-drained garden soil, and a position in full sun are needed.
Propagation: During spring, take 7.5-10cm (3-4in) long cuttings from side-shoots, insert them into pots of equal parts of peat and sharp sand and place these in a cold frame. Pot up the cuttings when rooted, and eventually set them in a nursery bed for three or four years, until they are large enough to be planted in the garden.

Above: **Cytisus x beanii**
This dwarf broom is ideal where it can tumble over rocks or dry stone walls and display its pea-shaped yellow flowers in late spring and early summer. It delights in a sunny position and well-drained but not very rich soil.

Cytisus x beanii

Broom (UK and USA)

A beautiful hybrid broom, this is a semi-prostrate deciduous shrub. During late spring and early summer, its yellow pea-like flowers are produced in ones, twos or threes on the previous year's shoots. The leaves are narrow, hairy and mid-green.
Height: 45-60cm (1½-2ft)
Spread: 75-90cm (2½-3ft)
Cultivation: Well-drained garden soil in full sun is best. Do not plant this cytisus in rich soil. Always use pot-grown plants, because it dislikes root disturbance. No regular pruning is needed.
Propagation: During late summer, take 5-9cm (2-3½in) long heel cuttings, inserting them into equal parts peat and sharp sand. Place the pots in a cold frame and, when the cuttings are rooted, pot them up into a sandy loam-based compost. Plunge the pots into a sheltered part of the garden and plant them out either in late spring or early autumn.

Chamaecyparis pisifera 'Filifera Aurea' is suitable for a prime position in a heather garden. Its strong colour, attractive foliage shape and eventual size make it an ideal focal point.

Cytisus x beanii is ideal for bringing colour and height to a rock garden. When trailing over a dry-stone wall, it relieves the flatness of its top. Retaining walls alongside paths often present the best sites.

ROCK AND NATURALIZED GARDENS

Eranthis hyemalis

Winter Aconite (UK and USA)

This distinctively-flowered, tuberous-rooted plant blooms late in winter, often amid snow. The 2.5cm (1in) wide, buttercup-like, lemon-yellow flowers appear with a ruff of pale green leaves. They are borne on stiff, near upright stems which rise from pale green and deeply-cut leaves.

Height: 10cm (4in)

Spread: 7.5-10cm (3-4in)

Cultivation: Winter Aconite needs a well-drained but moisture-retentive soil in full sun or partial shade. Heavy loams often provide the best conditions. Set the tubers 2.5cm (1in) deep in late summer.

Propagation: Lift the tubers as soon as the plant dies down and cut them into sections. Replant 7.5cm (3in) apart. Alternatively, sow fresh seed in seed compost. It also produces self-sown seedlings that can be replanted.

Erythronium tuolumnense

This beautiful corm-bearing plant has nodding, yellow, turk's-cap flowers during late spring. Each flower has six-pointed petals. The bright green, glossy, spatula-shaped leaves arise from soil-level, and provide a superb background for the yellow flowers.

Height: 15-30cm (6-12in)

Spread: 13-15cm (5-6in)

Cultivation: Fertile, moisture-retentive soil with a north-facing slope is best. Plant the corms in late summer. It is essential that the soil does not dry out. To ensure this, add peat, leafmould or garden compost before planting.

Propagation: It can be raised from seed, but this method often takes several years to produce flowering plants. The best way for home gardeners to increase this plant is by removing offsets in summer as the leaves die down. Put the offsets in a nursery bed for a few years until they reach flowering size, then plant them out.

Eranthis hyemalis is ideal for a corner in the rock garden, perhaps among stone chippings which help to prevent soil being splashed on them during heavy rain storms. Eranthis mixes well with Snowdrops (*Galanthus hyemalis*).

Erythronium tuolumnense is a wild garden plant, blending well with Wake Robin (*Trillium grandiflorum*) and the *Rhododendron* 'Blue Tit' which has lovely funnel-shaped lavender-blue flowers.

Left: **Eranthis hyemalis**
This ground-hugging tuberous plant has distinctive large, buttercup-like flowers with ruffs of pale green leaves. It grows best in heavy loams which do not dry out in spring or summer.

Euryops acraeus

A beautiful miniature evergreen shrub from the Drakensberg Mountains in Lesotho, southern Africa, euryops is an upright plant, densely clothed in summer in bright silver leaves and pure gold daisy-like flowers on short grey stems. It is often wrongly called *Euryops evansii.* It was once thought to be tender and was restricted to alpine houses. However, it will grow perfectly well in a well-drained site in a rock-garden.

Height: 25-30cm (10-12in
Spread: 45-60cm (1½-2ft)
Cultivation: Euryops likes ordinary well-drained garden soil and a position in full sun.
Propagation: Cuttings of non-flowering shoots can be taken in summer and inserted in sandy compost. However, it is easier and quicker to detach suckers from around the base of the plant. Pot them up in a well-drained sandy compost and place the pots in a cold frame until the plants are large enough to be set out in the garden.

Far-left: **Erythronium tuolumnense**
This corm-bearing plant delights in moist soil and shade, producing yellow flowers in late spring. It likes to be left undisturbed, so a wild garden setting is best. It can be planted in an informal group with other erythroniums.

Left: **Euryops acraeus**
This beautiful low-growing evergreen shrub for the rock garden has silvery foliage. The large, pure-gold, daisy-like flowers appear during summer, forming a handsome combination with the striking leaves.

Euryops acraeus grows well in hot places: a scree-bed on a hot, dry slope suits it well, and its silvery foliage is highlighted by the stone chippings. The foliage is also attractive when set with dark-green-leaved plants.

Genista lydia

Bulgarian Broom (UK)

A hummock-forming dwarf deciduous shrub. During late spring and early summer, it has bright golden-yellow, pea-shaped flowers on arching or prostrate, slender, five-angled, glabrous green shoots. The grey-green leaves are very narrow. It is ideal for a large rock garden, or for trailing over banks and low walls.

Height: 60-90cm (2-3ft)

Spread: 1.2-1.8m (4-6ft)

Cultivation: Genista does well in well-drained light soil in full sun, but it even succeeds in poor soils.

Propagation: During late summer, take 5-7.5cm (2-3in) long heel cuttings and insert them into pots of equal parts peat and sharp sand. Place these in a cold frame. When the plants are rooted, pot them up into free-draining sandy compost and plunge the pot in soil in a well-drained corner of the garden. Plant into the garden in autumn or spring.

Right: **Genista lydia**
The beautiful pea-shaped, golden-yellow flowers appear in late spring and early summer on this low-growing deciduous shrub. It is well suited to a large rock garden.

Left: **Genista pilosa prostrata**
This useful prostrate deciduous shrub has ground-hugging shoots, and small broom-like yellow flowers in late spring and early summer. It is essential to provide free-draining soil and a sunny position.

Genista pilosa

This distinguished, ground-hugging, deciduous shrub has procumbent shoots when young, later becoming an attractive tangled mass of slender twiggy shoots. During late spring and early summer, it reveals small pea-shaped yellow flowers. A prostrate, ground-hugging form is also available which grows no more

Genista lydia looks best when cascading over a low wall, perhaps from a high position on a rock garden. Set colourful and low growing plants, such as helianthemums and campanulas, beneath its waterfall-like shoots.

Genista pilosa is a delight when set at the top of a low wall where its shoots can trail over the top. Plant small dry-wall plants below it to continue the interest and colour for a longer period.

Genista sagittalis

(Chamaespartium sagittale)
This curious and unusual hardy shrub acquires the character of an evergreen plant from its unusual winged branches. The leaves themselves are scattered and few. Small, yellow, pea-like flowers appear in summer. It is an excellent ground-cover plant.
Height: 10-15cm (4-6in)
Spread: 45-60cm (1½-2ft)
Cultivation: Most garden soils suit it, as long as they are well-drained, light and in a sunny position, but it will even grow in poor soils. No pruning is needed, other than the occasional cutting back of intrusive shoots.
Propagation: During summer, take soft cuttings, inserting them around the edge of a 13-15cm (5-6in) clay pot containing a mixture of four parts sharp sand and one part peat. Next spring, when they are rooted, pot them up and plant out the following autumn.

Below: **Genista sagittalis**
This excellent prostrate shrub produces pea-like yellow flowers in summer. Its winged shoots are an attractive bonus, with the true leaves scattered and few, and small and hairy when young.

than 7.5cm (3in) high, and 90cm-1.2m (3-4ft) wide. Both types are ideal for a rock garden.
Height: 38-45cm (15-18in)
Spread: 60-90cm (2-3ft)
Cultivation: Any ordinary garden soil that is not too rich and has good drainage is suitable. Choose a sunny position. Cut out congested shoots after flowering.
Propagation: During late summer, take 5-7.5cm (2-3in) long heel cuttings and insert them into pots of equal parts peat and sharp sand. Place these in a cold frame. When the cuttings are rooted, pot them up into free-draining sandy compost and plunge the pots in soil in a well-drained corner of the garden. During autumn or spring, set the plants in the garden.

Genista sagittalis is ideal as a ground-cover shrub, filling large spaces between rocks. Another ground-hugging shrub is *Genista delphinensis*, the most prostrate of all brooms, only 2.5-5cm (1-2in) high, with bright yellow flowers in mid-summer.

ROCK AND NATURALIZED GARDENS

Juniperus communis 'Depressa Aurea'

This is a dwarf, wide-spreading and prostrate evergreen conifer with needle-like foliage. In spring, the leaves are bright butter-yellow, remaining golden throughout summer and dulling to bronze in autumn. In ten years it will grow 30cm (1ft) high and 1.2m (3ft) wide.
Height: 30-45cm (1-1½ft)
Spread: 2.4-3m (8-10ft)
Cultivation: This juniper needs good, well-drained soil in full sun. Like all golden-leaved conifers, it requires good light to ensure that the foliage remains bright.
Propagation: During late summer, take heel cuttings 5-10cm (2-4in)

Above: **Iris innominata**
This rhizome-bearing perennial iris prefers humus-rich soil, it dislikes lime. Flower colour can vary from plant to plant. Selected forms are best increased by division of the underground rhizomes.

Iris innominata

This rhizome-bearing iris comes originally from North America. Its long, narrow, dark green leaves are evergreen, and the stems bear one or two beardless flowers during early and mid-summer. They are 5-6.5cm (2-2½in) wide and in a range of colours, including cream, buff, yellow and orange. The plant forms a wide-spread clump.
Height: 15-25cm (6-10in)
Spread: 25-38cm (10-15in)
Cultivation: This plants delights in neutral or slightly acid soil, thriving in a peat bed. It also grows well in a pocket of fertile and humus-rich soil in a rock garden. It will do well in full sun or light shade.
Propagation: Sow seeds in autumn or spring in a loam-based seed compost, keeping them at 7°C (45°F). Prick out the seedlings into small pots. Use small plants, because large ones do not transplant easily. Particularly good forms can be increased by detaching pieces of the rhizomes in autumn.

Iris innominata needs a roomy site in the rock garden. Setting stone chippings around the plant shows off the attractive dark green and narrow leaves. Do not set other plants too close, or they may spoil its rounded shape.

Juniperus communis 'Depressa Aurea' is well suited to a rock garden. If positioned at the bottom of a slight slope, its beautiful foliage can be admired from above; planted by the side of a pond, it is a delight.

long, inserting them into pots of equal parts peat and sharp sand. Place these in a cold frame until the plants are rooted, then set them out in a nursery bed for a couple of years before planting them in the garden. When setting them out, remember that ultimately they will have a wide spread. Do not position them where they will eventually have to be pruned severely and their shape ruined.

Below: **Juniperus communis 'Depressa Aurea'**
A prostrate juniper with golden foliage, its shoots spread out just above soil-level, forming a dense shrub. In time it forms a golden carpet up to 3m (10ft) wide.

Above: **Juniperus x media 'Old Gold'**
A well-known, wide-spreading, slow-growing conifer, this variety retains its golden foliage throughout the year. Its ascending branches give it the appearance of a golden explosion.

Juniperus x media 'Old Gold'

This is an old and trusted semi-prostrate compact evergreen conifer. It has golden scale-like leaves which remain bright throughout the year. In ten years, it should reach 70cm (28in) high and 1.5m (5ft) wide.
Height: 1.8m (6ft)
Spread: 2.4m (8ft)
Cultivation: Well-drained garden soil and a position in full sun or slight shade are required. Good light ensures continuity of golden foliage throughout the year. It is a distinctive conifer and should not be cramped by other plants.
Propagation: During late summer, take heel cuttings 5-10cm (2-4in) long, inserting them into pots of equal parts peat and sharp sand. Place these in a cold frame until the cuttings are rooted, then set them out in nursery beds for a couple of years before planting them in their final positions.

Juniperus x media 'Old Gold' is superb for a junction between two paths or for creating a focal point in a heather garden. Its foliage also contrasts handsomely with paving slabs on a patio.

ROCK AND NATURALIZED GARDENS

Narcissus bulbocodium

Hoop Petticoat Daffodil (UK and USA)

This is a delicate bulbous plant with funnel-shaped, crinoline-like yellow flower trumpets, 2.5cm (1in) wide. These have tapering and slightly spiky petals. These appear during late winter and early spring. It is especially useful for naturalizing in an alpine meadow among fine grasses. Alternatively, it can be grown in soil pockets in a rock garden.

Height: 10-15cm (4-6in)
Spread: 10-13cm (4-5in)
Cultivation: Free-draining but moisture-retentive soil and slight shade are needed. Avoid soils which dry out in spring. Set the bulbs in holes three times their own depth in late summer. If setting them in grass, first spread out the bulbs irregularly on the grass and plant them where they lie. This helps to create a natural arrangement.
Propagation: Congested clumps can be lifted and replanted every three or four years.

Narcissus cyclamineus

This eye-catching miniature narcissus has bright, rich-yellow, tube-like trumpets, and petals completely swept back. It flowers in late winter and early spring. Like *Narcissus bulbocodium*, it can be naturalized in short, fine grass, or planted in sheltered corners in a rock garden.

Height: 15-20cm (6-8in)
Spread: 10cm (4in)
Cultivation: This narcissus prefers a moist, but not waterlogged, soil in slight shade. Plant the bulbs in late summer, setting them in holes three times their own depth.
Propagation: Lift, divide and replant congested clumps in summer, but do not thin out the bulbs too much; dominant clumps look best.

Narcissus bulbocodium can be harmonized with other spring-flowering plants, such as the Winter-flowering Jasmine (*Jasminium nudiflorum*) and the early spring purplish-pink *Rhododendron* 'Tessa'.

Narcissus cyclamineus is attractive when planted in short grass, with random clumps of a pink winter-flowering heather set behind it. Varieties of *Erica herbacea* (*E. carnea*) are ideal choices for this purpose.

Left: Narcissus bulbocodium
This is the Hoop Petticoat Daffodil, a small, delicate bulb with late winter and early spring flowers which resemble crinolines. It is excellent for naturalizing in areas covered by short, fine grass.

Right: Portulaca grandiflora
This beautiful rock garden or border flower is ideal for poor, dry soils. During summer, it displays saucer-shaped flowers in a range of colours, including yellow.

Below: Narcissus cyclamineus
A distinctive early, spring-flowering dwarf narcissus, ideal for naturalizing in short grass. It also does well alongside streams.

Portulaca grandiflora

Sun Plant (UK)
Rose Moss · Sun Plant ·
Eleven-O'Clock (USA)

An unusual, half-hardy succulent annual, the Sun Plant has narrow, fleshy, cylindrical bright green leaves and semi-prostrate, sprawling reddish stems. From early to late summer, it bears 2.5cm (1in) wide saucer-shaped red, purple or yellow flowers with bright yellow stamens. There are several varieties, extending the colour range to pink, crimson, orange and white. The F1 forms display double, rose-like flowers. It is ideal for a rock garden or border, and is also useful for filling gaps in any sunny position.
Height: 15-23cm (6-9in)
Spread: 6-20cm (6-8in)
Cultivation: Well-drained — even poor — soil and a sunny position are essential.
Propagation: During late winter and early spring, sow seeds 3mm (⅛in) deep in pots of loam-based compost, keeping them at 16°C (61°F). When the seedlings are large enough to handle, prick them out into boxes of loam-based compost and slowly harden them off in a cold frame. Set the plants in the garden in late spring, when all risk of frost has passed.

Above: Solidago brachystachys
This unusual miniature Golden Rod, rarely exceeds 15cm (6in) high, with golden-yellow flowers held in clusters during late summer and early autumn.

Alternatively, sow seeds 6mm (¼in) deep in late spring where the plants are to flower. Thin out the seedlings to 15cm (6in) apart.

Solidago brachystachys

(Solidago cutleri)
Dwarf Golden Rod (UK)

This unusual, hardy herbaceous Golden Rod has mid-green, lance-shaped leaves and golden-yellow flowers borne in clusters during late summer and into early autumn. Its low, slightly sprawling nature makes it ideal for a rock garden.
Height: 15cm (6in)
Spread: 30-38cm (12-15in)
Cultivation: Any good garden soil will do, but it must be well drained and in sun or slight shade.
Propagation: During spring lift and divide established clumps. Replant the young pieces from around the outside, discarding old parts. They will produce self-sown seedlings, but avoid growing these as they do not resemble the parents.

Portulaca grandiflora is superb as a ground-cover plant, with plants set among them to give added interest and height. *Kochia scoparia*, Summer Cypress, is ideal as a 'dot' plant because its foliage does not compete with the colourful flowers.

Solidago brachystachys does well with a sprinkling of stone chippings around it. This helps to prevent soil splashing on to the foliage during heavy rain storms, as well as creating an attractive and interesting background.

Sternbergia lutea

Yellow Star Flower · Winter Daffodil · Lily of the Field (UK) Winter Daffodil · Lily of the Field (USA)

This well-known bulb-bearing rock-garden plant bears goblet-shaped, shining waxy-yellow flowers up to 5cm (2in) long, in late summer and into early autumn. The strap-shaped, deep green leaves remain small and immature until the following spring.

Height: 10-15cm (4-6in)
Spread: 10-13cm (4-5in)
Cultivation: Well-drained soil and a sunny position are needed. Leave the bulbs undisturbed for as long as possible. Set new bulbs 10-15cm (4-6in) deep in late summer.
Propagation: Lift congested clumps in late summer, dividing and replanting them as soon as possible. Offset bulbs often take two years before producing flowers.

Taxus baccata 'Repens Aurea'

This is a low, prostrate, slow-growing evergreen conifer with dense foliage. Each leaf is green, with gold edges. The gold is pale in spring, gradually deepening during summer. The spreading branches have attractive drooping tips. In ten years, it will have grown about 35cm (4ft) high and 1m (3½ft) wide.

Height: 90cm (3ft)
Spread: 3m (10ft)
Cultivation: Well-drained soil in full sun suits it best. Indeed, if grown in shade, it soon loses its beautiful colour, so ensure it gets plenty of light.
Propagation: During late summer or early autumn, take 7.5-10cm (3-4in) long heel cuttings. Insert them into equal parts peat and sharp sand and place these in a cold frame. When the cuttings are rooted, plant them out in a nursery bed for a couple of years before setting them in the garden.

Above: **Sternbergia lutea**
A distinctive late-flowering bulb, which looks like a crocus and produces a welcome display of brilliant yellow flowers, it is ideal for bringing late colour to the corner of a rock garden.

Below: **Taxus baccata 'Repens Aurea'**
It is essential that this attractive prostrate yew with bright green and gold foliage is planted in full sun if it is to keep its bright variegated colouring.

Sternbergia lutea, with its dominantly-coloured flowers, needs to be set in a passive, non-conflicting setting. A backcloth of green or grey foliage will provide the right setting.

Taxus baccata 'Repens Aurea' needs a neighbour of contrasting colour and shape. Blue or dark-green foliaged conifers are best; if you want this golden yew to have a domed appearance, trim it with shears.

Thuja orientalis 'Aurea Nana'

This attractively rounded, slow-growing, evergreen dwarf conifer has vertical plates of yellow-green, scale-like leaves which turn gold in winter. In ten years it will reach 60cm (2ft) high, with a spread of 50cm (20in).
Height: 1m (3½ft)
Spread: 75-90cm (2½-3ft)
Cultivation: Deep, moist but not continually saturated garden soil, and a position in full sun assure success. In shady areas it will be a disappointment, with dull green foliage instead of yellow.
Propagation: During late summer or early autumn, take 5-10cm (2-4in) long cuttings, inserting them into pots of equal parts peat and sharp sand. Place these in a cold frame and, when the cuttings are rooted, plant them out in a nursery bed for a couple of years before transferring them to the garden.

Above: **Thuja orientalis 'Aurea Nana'**
This beautifully-shaped, slow-growing compact conifer has yellow-green scale-like leaves which turn gold in winter. It needs full sun to keep its colouring.

Below: **Thuja plicata 'Rogersii'**
This beautiful dwarf conifer has dense foliage, green with golden edges. In winter, this turns bronze and remains attractive throughout that too often dull period.

Thuja plicata 'Rogersii'

This dwarf slow-growing conical evergreen conifer has a lovely yellow glow. The fine foliage is packed in tight green clusters, with the edges of the scale-like leaves a rich golden-yellow. In winter the leaves become bronze. It is ideal for rock gardens, scree beds and for mixing in heather collections. It is so slow-growing that in ten years it will reach only 70cm (28in) high and 40cm (16in) wide.
Height: 1m (3½ft)
Spread: 90cm (3ft)
Cultivation: Ordinary garden soil is suitable, but it must not become dry during summer. A sheltered position in full sun also suits it.
Propagation: During late summer or early autumn, take 5-10cm (2-4in) long cuttings and put them into pots of equal parts peat and sharp sand. Place these in a cold frame and, when the cuttings are rooted, plant them out into a nursery bed for a couple of years before you set them in the garden.

Thuja orientalis 'Aurea Nana' is excellent for a rock garden or small heather collection. Prostrate conifers with colour-contrasting colours can be set near it. In a rock garden, small spring bulbs give added interest.

Thuja plicata 'Rogersii' looks especially good when set with stone chippings around it. The changing light patterns of the chippings pick up the colours in the thuja. This is especially effective in full sun.

ROCK AND NATURALIZED GARDENS

Tulipa tarda

(Tulipa dasystemon)

This eye-catching species tulip has narrow mid-green leaves, developing in a rosette from soil level. It bears up to five flowers on each stem. They have star-shaped, pointed yellow petals with white edges, up to 4cm (1½in) long. This tulip is ideal at the front of a border or in a rock garden.
Height: 15cm (6in)
Spread: 7.5cm (3in)
Cultivation: Well-drained soil and a sheltered position, preferably in good light and facing south, are most suitable. The bulbs can be left in the soil, but remember to remove the leaves as soon as they have died down.
Propagation: Congested clumps can be lifted and divided in autumn, replanting the bulbs 15cm (6in) deep and 7.5-10cm (3-4in) apart.

Above: **Tropaeolum polyphyllum**
This spectacular, tuberous-rooted rock garden plant from South America has long stems clothed in grey leaves and yellow flowers during mid-summer. It tends to die down when flowering is over.

Tropaeolum polyphyllum

This distinctive tuberous-rooted, ground-hugging herbaceous perennial has lobed grey-green leaves on arching stems. The large, rich yellow flowers, 12mm (½in) wide, appear on stems arising from the leaf joints during early and mid-summer. The whole plant often dies down after flowering, and is likely to come up in a different position the following year.
Height: 7.5-10cm (3-4in)
Spread: 90cm-1.2m (3-4ft)
Cultivation: Plant the tubers during spring, in friable soil, at a depth of 25-30cm (10-12in). Position them so that the plants will trail naturally, preferably over a large rock. It delights in a warm and sunny position, although it also grows in light shade.
Propagation: Once established, propagation is very easy. Just dig up the tubers in spring, replanting them before they dry out.

Tulipa sylvestris

This bulbous, easily-grown tulip species has narrow grey-green leaves and scented yellow flowers, 5cm (2in) wide. The reflexed petals make the flowers appear even larger than they are. Flowering is during mid-spring. These tulips are suitable for rock gardens and borders, and for naturalizing in woodland and grass.
Height: 30-38cm (12-15in)
Spread: 10-15cm (4-6in)
Cultivation: Well-drained soil, a sheltered site and a sunny south-facing position are ideal. Plant the bulbs in late summer or early autumn.
Propagation: You can raise plants from seed, but it is easier to increase from offsets.

Left: **Tulipa sylvestris**
An easily-grown species with beautiful scented yellow flowers, this tulip is ideal for rock gardens and borders, as well as for naturalizing in woodland and grass.

Below: **Tulipa tarda**
This small tulip is ideal for a rock garden. It needs an open and sunny position, where the flowers will open wide in good light. Up to five are produced on each stem.

Tropaeolum polyphyllum comes into its own when allowed to creep over large rocks and eventually tumble into space. It is ideal for covering wide-topped walls, especially soil-retaining types.

Tulipa tarda associates well with many plants: in the rock garden with the Pasque Flower (*Pulsatilla vulgaris*), and in the border with Crown Imperial (*Fritillaria imperialis*) and mauve-flowered violas.

Above: **Verbascum x 'Letitia'**
This beautiful hybrid was discovered in the British Royal Horticultural Society's Garden at Wisley in the early 1960s. The clear yellow flowers appear from mid-summer onwards.

Verbascum x 'Letitia'

A pretty hybrid between *V. dumulosum* and *V. spinosum*, with a twiggy but compact habit, it has velvety, grey-green lance-shaped leaves and numerous clear yellow flowers, 2.5cm (1in) wide, from mid-summer onwards.
Height: 25-38cm (10-15in)
Spread: 38-45cm (15-18in)
Cultivation: This lovely plant needs a sandy, well-drained soil in full sun. It dislikes continual dampness during winter and may require protection with panes of glass. It is ideal for scree beds and dry stone walls. It is also suitable for growing in an alpine house where it will thrive in a pot on a gravel-covered bench.
Propagation: The easiest way to increase it is by taking 5cm (2in) long heel cuttings during early summer, inserting them in pots of equal parts peat and sharp sand. Place them in a cold frame.

Further plants to consider

Draba bryoides imbricata
Height: 5-6.5cm (2-2½in)   Spread: 4-5cm (1½-2in)
An attractive, compact, hardy herbaceous perennial for the rock garden, with small cross-shaped golden-yellow flowers in spring.

Fritillaria pallidiflora
Height: 25-30cm (10-12in)   Spread: 10-15cm (4-6in)
An unusual fritillaria, with 4cm (1½in) long bell-shaped yellow flowers during spring.

Halimium ocymoides
(Helianthemum algarvense)
Height: 60-90cm (2-3ft)   Spread: 90cm-1.2m (3-4ft)
A beautiful compact shrub suitable for large rock gardens, where it reveals 2.5cm (1in) wide, bright yellow flowers with chocolate blotches in mid-summer.

Hypericum polyphyllum
Height: 15cm (6in)   Spread: 25-30cm (10-30in)
A low-growing shrubby perennial, with 4cm (1½in) wide golden flowers from mid to late summer. The form 'Sulphureum' bears pale yellow flowers.

Morisia monanthos
Height: 2.5cm (1in)   Spread: 10-15cm (4-6in)
A beautiful, low herbaceous perennial, with cross-shaped golden-yellow flowers, 12mm (½in) wide, forming clusters during spring and early summer.

Ranunculus gramineus
Height: 25-30cm (10-12in)   Spread: 20-25cm (8-10in)
A pretty member of the buttercup family, ideal for damp corners in a wild garden. From early to mid-summer it bears citron-yellow flowers. The foliage is narrow and glaucous-blue.

Roscoea cautleoides
Height: 30-38cm (12-15in)   Spread: 25-30cm (10-12in)
A hardy herbaceous perennial, with pale yellow, orchid-like flowers, 4-5cm (1½-2in) long, in mid-summer.

Uvularia perfoliata
Throat-wort (UK)
Height: 20-25cm (8-10in)   Spread: 15-20cm (6-8in)
A pretty rhizome-bearing perennial for a rock garden or peat bed. In late spring it produces many bell-shaped, pendant, pale-yellow flowers, singly or in pairs.

Waldsteinia fragarioides
Height: 13-20cm (5-8in)   Spread: 25-30cm (10-12in)
A strawberry-like North American plant, ideal for a large rock garden. During early summer it bears small, five-petalled, golden-yellow flowers above three-lobed, strawberry-like leaves.

Verbascum x 'Letitia' delights in a sunny position, especially one with good drainage such as the top of a dry stone wall. Its compact nature helps to interrupt the flatness of many such walls, and provides colour.

CHAPTER THREE

CONTAINER GARDENING

Houses and patios with flowers growing in window-boxes, in tubs, hanging baskets and other containers are rather like cakes with large glossy cherries on top; the container displays are the first features to capture attention. They sparkle and show off their colours.

Few containers are successful planted solely with single-colour flowers; usually, a colourful, bright mixture looks best. However, certain colours can be the key to an impressive display, where they are highlighted by their backgrounds. Strong yellows look extra bright and distinguished against white backgrounds. Zinnias and marigolds interplanted with dark red geraniums are a delight against white walls. Another combination is the pouched bright yellow flowers of calceolarias and mixed colours of Iceland Poppies grown as half-hardy annuals in containers. Trailing nasturtiums and Creeping Jenny (*Lysimachia nummularia*) are splendid at the front of containers where they extend the vertical display.

Dark backgrounds also show off yellow flowers to advantage, but then the containers are best painted white to give extra contrast. Yellow dwarf wallflowers and colour-contrasting Parrot Tulips make a fine spring display in containers. White tubs and strong plastic white urns are distinctive when placed either side of an entrance and planted with yellow flowers.

Yellow-foliaged conifers are a continuing delight throughout the year and especially during winter. Again, they look good in pairs, either side of an entrance. Even small trees can be grown in large containers on a patio. *Acer japonicum* 'Aureum', with bright yellow foliage turning reddish-crimson in autumn, is ideal for a large patio.

For plants which are permanent features in large tubs, it may be necessary to place plastic over the soil during wet winter months to prevent the compost becoming too wet. When covered, check the compost regularly, especially in spring, to ensure it has not become too dry; moisten it if necessary.

Left: **Hanging baskets** *are superb for creating colour at eye-height and are especially valuable in small gardens or on patios.*

CONTAINER GARDENING

Coreopsis tinctoria

(Coreopsis bicolor)

This is one of the best known hardy annuals, bringing a profusion of colour to the garden from mid to late summer. The 5cm (2in) wide, daisy-shaped, bright yellow flowers are borne on stiff stems. The plant is just as good in containers on a patio as in the garden with other annuals. However, the dwarf varieties, at 23-30cm (9-12in), are better in containers than the taller types, at 60-90cm (2-3ft). 'Dwarf Dazzler' at 30cm (1ft) and 'Dwarf Mixed' at 23cm (9in) are best in containers, while 'All Double Mixed' and 'Single Mixed' at 75-90cm (2½-3ft) are best in a border. The lower ones can be used in borders, but towards the front.
Height: 23-90cm (9in-3ft) range
Spread: 15-25cm (6-10in) range
Cultivation: Well-drained fertile soil in a sunny position ensures success; this is a particularly good plant for town gardens.
Propagation: When grown in a hardy annual border, sow seeds thinly in drills during spring and early summer in the positions where the plants are to flower. When they are large enough to handle, thin out the seedlings. However, when grown for use in containers, sow seeds in early

Chrysanthemum parthenium

(Matricaria eximia)
Feverfew (UK and USA)

This hardy herbaceous perennial is grown as an annual, with pungent light green leaves and small white flowers, 18mm (¾in) wide, from mid to late summer. Several old and trusted varieties are available, such as 'Golden Ball' which grows to 25cm (10in) and has golden-yellow double flowers on compact plants. 'Snow Ball' is another good variety, up to 30cm (1ft) high, with masses of ivory-white double flowers. 'Gold Star' at 20cm (8in) has yellow-centred flowers, surrounded by white petals. Other varieties reach 75cm (2½ft), but it is the low-growing types that are best for border edging and containers such as tubs, troughs and window-boxes.
Height: 23-75cm (9in-2½ft)
Spread: 23-60cm (9in-2ft)
Cultivation: Feverfew likes well-drained, fertile, light soil in full sun or slight shade. In containers, use

Above: **Chrysanthemum parthenium 'Golden Ball'**
This is a useful compact annual for the edges of borders and tubs, as well as window-boxes and troughs. The bright button-like flowers bring life to the garden.

a good loam-based compost and, to encourage bushiness, nip out the initial flower buds.
Propagation: To produce plants for growing in containers, sow seeds 3mm (⅛in) deep in trays of loam-based seed compost in late winter or early spring. Keep the trays at 15°C (59°F). As soon as the seedlings are large enough to handle, prick them off into boxes of loam-based compost and harden them off in a cold frame. Plant them out into the garden in late spring. Alternatively, sow seeds directly into the border where the plants are to flower. Make shallow drills in the soil during late spring, lightly covering the seeds. When large enough to handle, thin the seedlings to 25cm (10in) apart.

Chrysanthemum parthenium 'Golden Ball' suits formal bedding schemes, set as an edging to *Pelargonium* 'Masterpiece', with its double orange flowers and tricoloured foliage. For added height use *Senecio maritima* as a 'dot' plant.

Coreopsis tinctoria is available in a wide range of heights, suitable for a variety of positions: front and middle of borders, edging to paths and borders, and in containers. For a quick display, rapidly covering the soil, set the plants closer together.

spring in loam-based compost kept at 16°C (61°F). When the seedlings are large enough to handle, prick them out into pots, five to a 15cm (6in) container, and harden them off in a cold frame. Plant them into containers in the garden during late spring and early summer.

Left: **Coreopsis tinctoria 'Dwarf Dazzler'**
A beautiful and reliable dwarf form with golden and crimson flowers through much of summer, this is a useful plant for towns and cities with pollution problems.

Hypericum olympicum 'Citrinum'

This low-growing, deciduous, mound-like St. John's Wort develops 23-30cm (9-12in) high stems clothed with small, grey-green, narrowly oval or oblong stalkless leaves. The bright lemon-yellow five-petalled summer flowers, 5cm (2in) wide, have central bosses of long, spiky stamens. It is ideal for the corner of a stone sink, or in a rock garden. It is often wider-spreading than the figures given below; instead of being 45cm (1½ft) in breadth, it may after several years reach 90cm (3ft) wide. At the same time it forms a slightly higher mound. If plants in sink gardens do become too large, swamping other plants, transplant them to the border in mid to late spring when the soil is warming up.
Height: 23-30cm (9-12in)
Spread: 30-45cm (1-1½ft)
Cultivation: Well-drained fertile soil and a sunny position suit this plant.
Propagation: During early and mid-summer, take 5cm (2in) long cuttings, inserting them into pots of equal parts peat and sharp sand. Place these in a cold frame. When the cuttings have rooted, pot them up into pots of loam-based compost and overwinter in a cold frame. Transplant them into the garden during spring.

Above: **Hypericum olympicum 'Citrinum'** *The bright lemon-yellow flowers, 5cm (2in) wide, with large central bosses of spiky stamens, are a delight in summer. The flowers appear at the tops of leaf-clad stems.*

Hypericum olympicum 'Citrinum', with its strong yellow flowers, blends with the blue-flowered *Veronica prostrata*. Position it so that the blue flowers are next to the yellow ones of the hypericum.

CONTAINER GARDENING

Mesembryanthemum oculatus 'Lunette'

This beautiful early-flowering, low-growing, half-hardy annual boasts bright yellow daisy-like flowers with darker centres. The flowers appear earlier than those of *criniflorum* types, and under duller conditions. It is ideal for the front of window-boxes and in hanging-baskets.
Height: 7.5-10cm (3-4in)
Spread: 15-25cm (6-10in)
Cultivation: Well-drained light soil is best, and a position in full sun. In containers, use a sandy loam-based compost.
Propagation: During spring, sow seeds in trays of loam-based

Above: **Mesembryanthemum oculatus 'Lunette'**
A new, early-flowering, half-hardy annual, this variety is ideal for the edge of window-boxes and hanging-baskets. It is a bright and reliable plant.

compost kept at 18°C (65°C). After germination, prick off the seedlings into boxes or pots, and harden them off in a cold frame. Set the plants 20-23cm (8-9in) apart in the containers. Alternatively, if no heat is available sow seeds in the open soil where they are to flower during late spring, thinning the seedlings later. However, germination may not be rapid.

Mesembryanthemum oculatus 'Lunette' is ideal for filling bare patches in rock gardens, creating colour before the permanent plants are fully established. It gives good ground cover, and brings colour right up to the edges of rocks and paths.

Sedum spathulifolium

This North-west American perennial succulent plant will soon form a dense mat of foliage. The grey-green leaves, borne in fleshy rosettes, are covered during mid-summer with 5cm (2in) wide heads of bright yellow flowers on 10cm (4in) stems. The form 'Cape Blanco' displays silvery-grey foliage, while 'Purpureum' has large purple leaves. 'Aurea' has leaves tinted yellow. These plants can be used in sink gardens as well as rock gardens. *Sedum acre* 'Aureum', a form of the Biting Stonecrop, native to Western Europe, including Britain, is an invasive and mat-forming plant and is best grown in crevices in dry stone walls, where it produces a mass of small mid to yellow-green leaves. During mid-summer, it bears flattened 2.5-4cm (1-1½in) wide heads of golden-yellow star-like flowers. Its spreading and mat-forming growth habit can be used to create an attractive feature by planting it where it can spread — away from choice rock garden subjects — and underplanting it with miniature bulbs. *Sedum acre* is also known as the Wall-pepper, an indication of its natural home. done at almost any time, but spring is best. Alternatively, small pieces which break off soon produce roots when pushed into compost.

Height: 5-10cm (2-4in)
Spread: 23-30cm (9-12in)
Cultivation: Well-drained garden soil in full sun is best, and although all sedums are relatively drought-resistant, do not allow the soil to become rock hard.
Propagation: The easiest way to increase this plant is to divide congested clumps. This can be

Left: **Sedum spathulifolium 'Cape Blanco'**
A distinctive stonecrop, this has silvery-grey leaves and bright yellow flowers during mid-summer. Several other forms are available, with purple or yellow-tinted leaves.

Sedum spathulifolium 'Cape Blanco' can be used in a stone sink with several other plants, such as *Lithodora diffusa* with blue flowers, *Sedum cauticolum* with rosy-blush blooms, and *Sedum* 'Vera Jameson'.

Ursinia anethoides

This half-hardy perennial is usually grown as a half-hardy annual. It has daisy-like, brilliant orange-yellow flowers, 5cm (2in) wide, with central purple discs from early to late summer. Several superb varieties are available, including 'Sunstar' with deep orange flowers and dark red central discs, and 'Sunshine', with bright golden-yellow flowers and maroon discs. It does well in borders and containers.

Height: 38-45cm (15-18in)
Spread: 25-30cm (10-12in)
Cultivation: Light, relatively poor soil suits it best, and a position in full sun.
Propagation: During early spring, sow seeds 3mm (⅛in) deep in trays of loam-based compost kept at 15°C (59°C). When the seedlings are large enough to handle, prick them out into boxes and place them in a cold frame to harden off. In late spring, after all risk of frost has passed, plant them out into a container.

Above: **Ursinia anethoides** *This bright, half-hardy annual with golden-yellow flowers needs plenty of sunshine. It is admirable for bringing colour to hot, sunny patios and terraces, where its flowers create interest over a long period. Ursinias make excellent pot plants.*

Venidium fastuosum

Monarch of the Veldt (UK)
Cape Daisy (USA)

This superb half-hardy annual from South Africa brings colour to all gardens, whether in containers or in a border. It has deeply-lobed leaves and stems with a silvery-white texture, and large, rich orange daisy-like flowers, 10cm (4in) wide, from early to late summer. The inner edges of the petals are banded purple-brown, with a central black cone. They are ideal as cut flowers. Another species, *Venidium decurrens*, also native to South Africa, boasts beautiful, large-faced, daisy-like, dark-centred golden-yellow flowers up to 6.5cm (2½in) wide. It is really a half-hardy perennial but is invariably grown as an annual. Its flowers appear from mid-summer to early autumn on plants 25-30cm (10-12in) high and with a similar spread, with deeply-lobed greyish-

Ursinia anethoides is worth planting on its own in a large tub or low urn: its boldly-coloured and long-lasting flowers would dominate and subjugate plants set with it. However, in a border it can be planted in small groupings, with bold blues around it.

Above: **Tagetes patula** *Popularly known as French Marigolds, these favourite border flowers make a bold display of bright yellow.*

green leaves. Like *Venidium fastuosum*, it is ideal as a cut-flower for home decoration.
Height: 50-60cm (20-24in)
Spread: 30-38cm (12-15in)
Cultivation: Well-drained, fertile, light compost in containers or borders is essential, and a sunny position.
Propagation: Sow seeds thinly in boxes of loam-based compost during early spring. Keep them at 16°C (61°F). When the seedlings are large enough to handle, prick them out into boxes or pots of loam-based compost and harden them off in a cold frame before planting them in containers or a border in late spring, after all risk of frost damage has passed.

Left: **Venidium fastuosum**
The stunningly attractive 10cm (4in) wide flowers make an ideal feature for a container on a sunny patio or for a border. The flowers are also excellent for cutting for the house.

Further plants to consider

Calceolaria 'Fothergillii'

Slipper Flower (UK)   Slipperwort · Slipper Flower · Pocketbook Flower (USA)

Height: 15cm (6in)   Spread: 15-20cm (6-8in)
A hardy perennial, well suited to rock gardens or window-boxes, with yellow pouch-shaped flowers revealing purple-flecked throats. Two other low-growing forms are available: 'Golden Bunch' at 20cm (8in) with yellow flowers, and 'Midas' at 20cm (8in) with pure yellow flowers.

Erysimum alpinum
(Cheiranthus alpinus)

Alpine Wallflower · Fairy Wallflower (UK)

Height: 15cm (6in)   Spread: 10-15cm (4-6in)
A beautiful, diminutive hardy biennial that can be set at the edge of a stone sink to create extra 'instant' colour during early summer. The sulphur-yellow 12mm (½in) wide flowers are beautifully fragrant.

Petunia 'Summer Sun'

Height: 30-38cm (12-15in)   Spread: 30-38cm (12-15in)
Ideal for flowering in large containers on patios, displaying 5-6.5cm (2-2½in) wide yellow flowers.

Tagetes erecta 'Aztec Fire Mixed'

African Marigold

Height: 20-25cm (8-10in)   Spread: 25-30cm (10-12in)
A half-hardy annual, with flowers in shades of hot gold and grapefruit yellow from early summer onwards.

Tagetes patula 'Fireflame'

French Marigold

Height: 20-25cm (8-10in)   Spread: 25-30cm (10-12in)
An exceptionally beautiful, half-hardy, dwarf double French Marigold, with golden-yellow and red flowers. An even smaller variety is 'Gypsy Sunshine' at 15-20cm (6-8in) high, with warm butter-yellow flowers. An ultra dwarf single form is 'Teeny Weeny' at 13cm (5in), with red and yellow flowers.

Tagetes tenuifolia 'Lemon Gem'
(Tagetes signata)

Height: 23cm (9in)   Spread: 23-30cm (9-12in)
A beautiful, small, half-hardy annual with a neat, mound-like habit, clothed with lemon-yellow flowers from early summer onwards. 'Golden Gem', 15cm (6in) has golden flowers.

Zinnia 'Short Stuff'

Height: 15-18cm (6-7in)   Spread: 15-20cm (6-8in)
This hybrid is available in six different colours, including yellow. Its blooms are double, disease-resistant and ideal for containers.

Venidium fastuosum needs white or blue colour around it to show off its beautiful flowers. But remember to choose flowers that do not rise above and hide the rich orange blooms.

CHAPTER FOUR

WALL AND TRELLIS FILLERS

Gold and yellow are, to many people, magical colours, reflecting the sun and bringing life to a garden, particularly when seen against a sun-blessed wall. Good yellow and gold plants for filling walls and trelliswork are of many types. Black-eyed Susan (*Thunbergia alata*) is a bright-eyed half-hardy annual, while the Canary Creeper (*Tropaeolum peregrinum*) is a twining, half-hardy perennial grown as a half-hardy annual. *Humulus lupulus aureus*, a close cousin of the beer maker's hop, is an attractive herbaceous perennial, producing a fresh set of leaves each year.

Several yellow-flowered shrubs which grow well in a border or as specimen plants on a lawn can also be grown to advantage against a south or west-facing wall. Two such plants are the Moroccan Broom (*Cytisus battendieri*) and the Evergreen Laburnum (*Piptanthus laburnifolius*). They both welcome the extra warmth and protection provided by a wall.

There are a number of lovely yellow and gold climbing roses; the clear yellow flowers of *Rosa ecae* 'Helen Knight' are very eye-catching, particularly when planted in association with the Mountain Clematis (*Clematis montana*).

Traditionally, the honeysuckle family is first thought of when considering climbers, and any gardener would be delighted with the golden-yellow clusters of Chinese Honeysuckle (*Lonicera tragophylla*). From early winter to early spring, Winter-flowering Jasmine (*Jasminum nudiflorum*) delights with its bright yellow flowers borne on bare stems. It is not strictly a climber, but more of a 'leaner', so give it a framework to lean on, and tie it in regularly.

Heights and spreads given for the plants in this chapter are guides only, because the plant will adapt its growth if more space is available.

Left: **Lonicera tragophylla** *creates a strong impact during mid-summer with large clusters of golden flowers. Make sure its roots are in shade.*

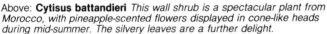

Above: **Cytisus battandieri** *This wall shrub is a spectacular plant from Morocco, with pineapple-scented flowers displayed in cone-like heads during mid-summer. The silvery leaves are a further delight.*

Cytisus battandieri

Moroccan Broom (UK)

This startlingly attractive deciduous or semi-evergreen shrub from the Atlas Mountains in Morocco is often grown as a free-standing shrub, and is ideal for south or west-facing walls. The pineapple-scented, golden-yellow mid-summer flowers are borne in 10cm (4in) long cone-like clusters during mid-summer. The large, grey, laburnum-like leaves are covered with silky-white hairs which give them a silvery appearance.
Height: 2.4-3.5m (8-12ft)
Spread: 2.4-3m (8-10ft)
Cultivation: Well-drained, deeply-cultivated neutral or slightly acid soil is best. Soils which are alkaline tend to make the plant short-lived. A south or west-facing wall is best. The shrub flowers on wood formed the previous season, so cut back the shoots after flowering to within a few inches of their bases. Do not cut into the old wood, as it may then not break into new growth.
Propagation: You can sow seeds in spring and raise the seedlings in a cold frame. Alternatively, take 7.5-10cm (3-4in) long heel cuttings in late summer. Insert them into pots containing equal parts of peat and sharp sand, and transfer to a cold frame. Pot up the cuttings, when rooted, into small pots of a peat-based compost and plant out into the garden in late summer.

Humulus lupulus aureus

This is an unusual herbaceous perennial climber with soft yellow three to five-lobed coarsely-toothed leaves, 10-15cm (4-6in) wide. It has stems which twine clockwise. It is especially useful for clothing garden features such as arches and pergolas, or perhaps trailing over a path and forming a tunnel of soft yellow leaves.
Height: 3-6cm (10-20ft)
Spread: 2.4-3.5m (8-12ft)
Cultivation: Fertile, moist but not waterlogged soil suits it best, and a position in full sun. In autumn, remove all dead foliage and cut the stems down to soil-level.

Cytissus battandieri, with its bright-yellow flowers, contrasts perfectly with the strong blue flowers of agapanthus set below it. Both these plants appreciate a warm, sunny position.

Humulus lupulus aureus soon takes to a trellis or pergola, but will also trail and climb through a neglected, sparse hedge, filling the gaps with its attractive yellow leaves.

Jasminum nudiflorum

Winter-flowering Jasmine · Winter Jasmine (UK)

This hardy deciduous shrub with long, whip-like stems is perhaps one of the best known winter-flowering shrubs, blooming from early winter often through to early spring. It has lustrous dark green leaves, each made up of three leaflets, and 18-25mm (¾-1in) wide, bright yellow star-shaped flowers, borne singly or in small clusters on shoots developed since the previous spring. During flowering, the shoots are bare of leaves. It is not strictly a climber, but a 'leaner' that needs support.

Height: 1.8-3m (6-10ft)
Spread: 1.8-2.4m (6-8ft)
Cultivation: This jasmine needs moderately fertile well-drained soil, preferably against an east or north-facing wall. The dainty flowers do not appear to be damaged by frost alone, but when frost is combined with early-morning sun, it causes damage. Because the flowers are produced on shoots developed since the previous spring, it can be pruned back hard in spring. Leave all the main shoots alone and just cut back the flowered shoots to two or three buds of their origin. This pruning encourages the development of side-shoots which will bear flowers the following winter. The new shoots will need tying-in to supports throughout the summer months.

Propagation: During late summer, take 7.5-10cm (3-4in) long semi-ripe cuttings; cut the lower ends just below a leaf-joint. Insert them into pots containing equal parts of peat and sharp sand, and keep at 7°C (45°F). When the cuttings are rooted, pot them up into 7.5cm (3in) pots of loam-based compost and put them in a cold frame. Alternatively, layer low-growing shoots in autumn. Rooting usually takes about a year.

Above: **Humulus lupulus aureus**
The soft yellow, three to five-lobed leaves of this herbaceous perennial form a dense screen, ideal for covering unsightly objects. In fertile, moist soil it soon becomes an eye-catching display.

Right: **Jasminum nudiflorum**
This winter-flowering shrub can be trained against a wall or allowed to sprawl up and over a low wall. The bright yellow, star-shaped flowers are borne singly or in small clusters along bare shoots.

Propagation: It can be increased from seed, but division of the rootstock in early autumn or spring is an easier method of propagation.

Jasminum nudiflorum looks good with another winter flowering plant, *Mahonia aquifolium*, which has terminal clusters of golden-yellow flowers. It also mixes with the violet and yellow *Iris histrioides*.

WALL AND TRELLIS FILLERS

Right: **Lonicera nitida 'Baggesen's Gold'**
Few golden-leaved plants are as eye-catching in full sun as this small-leaved, evergreen shrub. When planted against a wall or fence, it soon becomes a handsome screen.

Lonicera nitida 'Baggesen's Gold'

A densely-leaved evergreen shrub with 6mm (¼ in) long, golden-yellow leaves which turn yellow-green in autumn. It can be grown as a specimen shrub in a border, where its foliage has year-round interest. But it is best positioned against a sunny wall or unsightly shed or garage, where it soon forms an attractive screen.

Height: 1.5-1.8m (5-6ft)
Spread: 90cm-1.5m (3-5ft)
Cultivation: Lonicera likes a well-drained fertile soil in full sun. Good light enhances the attractive leaves and maintains their gold colouring. No regular pruning is needed, other than trimming it in spring to fill the space allotted to it. Although, like its parent form, it can be trimmed with shears, it is far better left with a more informal shape.
Propagation: An easy way is to layer low-growing shoots in late summer or early winter. They usually take about a year to develop roots. Also, hardwood cuttings, 20-25cm (8-10in) long, can be taken in late summer and inserted in a sheltered corner. These also take about a year to produce roots. Another way is to take 10cm (4in) long cuttings during mid to late summer, inserting them in pots containing equal parts of peat and sharp sand and placing them in a cold frame. Pot up the cuttings, when they are rooted, into a loam-based compost, and replace in the cold frame. Plant out in a nursery bed in spring until established, when they can be planted in their final sites in autumn or in the following spring. Choose a sunny position.

Lonicera tragophylla

Chinese Woodbine (UK)

A beautiful, vigorous, deciduous climber, ideal for fences, archways, pergolas and walls, this plant was introduced into cultivation in 1900 from its native Western China. During mid-summer, it displays large terminal clusters of scentless, bright golden-yellow flowers with trumpets up to 4cm (1½in) wide and tubes up to 7.5cm (3in) long.
Height: 4.5-6m (15-20ft)
Spread: 3-4.5m (10-15ft)
Cultivation: It delights in a position with a cool root-run. Well-drained relatively fertile soil is needed, with the foliage and flowers in full sun. No regular pruning is needed, other than cutting out dead wood after flowering.
Propagation: Seeds can be sown in loam-based compost when ripe in early autumn, and placed in a cold frame. Alternatively, take 7.5-10cm (3-4in) long cuttings in mid-summer. Insert them into pots containing equal parts of peat and sharp sand and place them in a cold frame. When rooted, pot up the cuttings and replace them in the cold frame.

Lonicera nitida 'Baggesen's Gold' is ideal for covering unsightly sheds or garages. Bulbs with strong blue flowers make a superb colour contrast set close to its base; Grape Hyacinths are ideal.

Piptanthus laburnifolius

(Piptanthus nepalensis)
Evergreen Laburnum

This is an unusual, slightly tender, almost evergreen shrub with dark green leaves formed of three lance-shaped leaflets, 7.5-15cm (3-6in) long. The pea-shaped, bright-yellow laburnum-like flowers, 4cm (1½in) long, appear in late spring and early summer. It can be grown in the open, but does better against a south or west-facing wall.

Height: 2.4-3-5m (8-12ft)
Spread: 1.8-3m (6-10ft)
Cultivation: Light, well-drained soil in a sheltered, warm position is essential. No regular pruning is needed, other than cutting out dead branches in spring. If the foliage has been badly damaged by frost, cut it back in spring.
Propagation: It is easily increased from seeds sown in early spring in peaty compost and placed in a cold frame. When large enough to handle, prick off the seedlings into small pots of loam-based compost. The plants can be set in a nursery bed in autumn, for a year or so. Alternatively, take 7.5-10cm (3-4in) long, half-ripe heel cuttings in late summer. When they are rooted, pot them up into small pots.

Above: **Lonicera tragophylla**
This vigorous climber is well suited to a large wall, in a position which gives it a cool root-run and plenty of sun for the foliage. Flowering is during mid-summer. It is best positioned where its roots are in shade, perhaps from a shrub.

Right: **Piptanthus laburnifolius**
This unusual, almost evergreen shrub bears pea-shaped, bright-yellow flowers in late summer. It can be grown as a specimen shrub, but is better against a warm wall. It will not live long in cold or very windy areas.

Lonicera tragophylla is ideal for trailing over a sparsely foliaged tree, a trellis or a pergola. The roots soon find the cool side of the tree, while the flowers climb into the sunlight.

WALL AND TRELLIS FILLERS

Rosa ecae 'Helen Knight'

A dainty, hardy, deciduous shrub rose, well-branched and prickly, with slender, pliable, arching reddish-brown stems. The small, fern-like leaves are formed of five to nine oval leaflets, with the clear yellow, saucer-shaped flowers, 5cm (2in) wide, borne freely during mid-summer.

Height: 1.5-2.1m (5-7ft)
Spread: 1.2-1.5m (4-5ft)
Cultivation: Ordinary well-drained garden soil, not too light is suitable. A position in full sun is essential, facing south or west. Little pruning is needed, other than thinning out congested wood and bare shoots during early spring — or late winter in mild areas.
Propagation: During late summer and early autumn, take 23cm (9in) long heel cuttings, or take cuttings just below a bud. Insert them in a sand-lined, straight-sided trench, so that two-thirds of each cutting is buried. Remove the lower leaves from the cuttings.

Right: **Rosa ecae 'Helen Knight'**
Few species roses for training against a wall are as attractive as this shrub, with 5cm (2in) wide, clear yellow flowers during mid-summer. It must have a sunny position to ensure success.

Left: **Thunbergia alata**
This bright half-hardy annual is ideal for a cool greenhouse but also excellent in a warm, sheltered and sunny position outdoors. The orange-yellow flowers, with dark purple-brown centres, appear from mid-summer to autumn.

Thunbergia alata

Clock Vine · Black-eyed Susan (UK)
Black-eyed Susan Vine (USA)

This extremely bright-flowered, half-hardy annual climber has stems which twine around its supports. It bears ovate light green leaves and orange-yellow flowers with dark purple-brown centres, 5cm (2in) wide, from mid-summer to autumn. It is ideal for a cool greenhouse, but also thrives outdoors if given a warm position.
Height: 1.2-1.8m (4-6ft)
Spread: 60-90cm (2-3ft)
Cultivation: Ordinary well-drained soil and a sunny, sheltered position are essential.
Propagation: In spring, sow seeds 6mm (¼in) deep, three seeds to a 7.5cm (3in) wide pot. Use loam-based compost and keep at 16°C (61°F). When the seedlings are growing well, slowly harden them off, setting the plants outside as soon as all risk of frost is over.

Rosa ecae 'Helen Knight' can be planted with *Clematis montana*. They flower at the same time, when the pure white clematis flowers mingle attractively with the yellow rose blooms.

Thunbergia alata can be grown on its own, but it is more attractive when allowed to climb among a blue-flowered clematis. If you grow it in a pot, make a tripod from bamboo canes for a support.

Above: **Tropaeolum peregrinum**
This beautiful half-hardy annual bears interestingly shaped canary-yellow flowers from mid-summer to autumn. The light green, five-lobed leaves provide an attractive foil for the dramatic flowers.

Tropaeolum peregrinum

(Tropaeolum canariense)
Canary Creeper (UK)
Canary-bird Flower · Canary-bird Vine · Canary Creeper (USA)

This rapid-growing, twining, half-hardy perennial is frequently grown as a half-hardy annual. It bears five-lobed blue-green leaves and canary-yellow, elegantly-fringed flowers, 1.8-2.5cm (¾-1in) wide and adorned with graceful green spurs, from mid-summer to autumn. It looks superb when planted in bold drifts in a border, or in hanging-baskets or window-boxes, where it can trail.
Height: 2.4-3.5m (8-12ft)
Spread: 75-90cm (2½-3ft)
Cultivation: Fertile, but not excessively rich soil in a warm and sunny position is best. The Canary Creeper also needs support from trelliswork or canes.
Propagation: During late winter and early spring, sow two seeds 12mm (½in) deep in a 7.5cm (3in) wide pot of loam-based compost. Keep the pot at 16°C (61°F). After germination, thin to one seedling per pot. Harden them off and plant them out into the garden in early summer, after all risk of frost damage has passed.

Further plants to consider

Clematis cirrhosa balearica

Fern-leaf Clematis (UK)

Height: 3.5-4.5m (12-15ft)
A daintily, evergreen, slender-stemmed climber with prettily divided leaves, tinged bronze in winter. The pale yellow flowers, 5cm (2in) wide, and spotted reddish-purple inside, appear throughout winter.

Clematis orientalis

Orange-peel Clematis (UK)

Height: 3-5.4m (10-18ft)
A vigorous, deciduous climber with a mass of tangled shoots, bearing slightly fragrant, bell-shaped, nodding yellow flowers, 5cm (2in) wide, during late summer and into autumn.

Clematis rehderana

Height: 4.5-6m (15-20ft)
A deciduous climber with coarsely-toothed leaflets and nodding, bell-shaped flowers during late summer and autumn. The flowers are a soft primrose yellow and are cowslip-scented.

Clematis tangutica

Height: 3-4.5m (10-15ft)
An attractive, deciduous, slender, vigorous climber with a rambling nature. It bears lantern-shaped, rich-yellow flowers in late summer and into autumn.

Hedera helix 'Goldheart'

Ivy

Height: 1.8-4.5m (6-15ft)   Spread: 1.8-2.4m (6-8ft)
A hardy, self-clinging climber with dark green leaves displaying dominant yellow central splashes. It produces its best colouring on south or west-facing walls, but will nevertheless survive the coldest of northerly aspects if required to.

Jasminum mesnyi

Primrose Jasmine (UK)   Japanese Jasmine · Primrose Jasmine · Yellow Jasmine (USA)

Height: 1.8-3m (6-10ft)
An evergreen climber, best suited to a south or west-facing wall in a warm area. During spring and into early summer, it bears 5cm (2in) wide, semi-double yellow flowers.

Pittosporum tobira

Japanese Pittosporum · Australian Laurel · Mock Orange · House-blooming Mock Orange (USA)

Height: 2.4-3.5m (8-12ft)
A slow-growing evergreen for sheltered, warm areas. From spring to mid-summer, it displays orange-blossom-scented, creamy-white flowers in terminal clusters. It needs the protection of a south or west-facing wall.

Tropaeolum peregrinum blends well in cottage-style gardens, but it also suits modern gardens, especially as a cloak for hiding ugly objects. For example, it will soon clothe a pole supporting a car-port.

CHAPTER FIVE

TREES AND SHRUBS

Trees and shrubs are the plants that provide permanency and continuity in a garden, establishing a framework around which other plants can be set. Some can also be used to form hedges, creating boundaries or separating small sections within the main part of the garden. Others, such as the profusely flowering *Genista cinerea*, can be used as specimen plants. From early to mid-summer, *Genista cinerea* produces a profusion of sweetly-scented yellow flowers.

Conifers with yellow foliage bring welcome splashes of colour to hedges and shrub borders, or golden-leaved privet can be planted in combination with the common green-leaved privet to form an unusual and eye-catching hedge. However, when doing this use two golden-leaved varieties between each green-leaved plant, because the latter is more vigorous and tends to suffocate its golden relative if used in equal proportions.

Yellow and golden-leaved shrubs are especially welcome in spring and early summer, when their fresh, rich colours are accentuated by the increasing intensity of the sunlight. The golden-leaved *Acer japonicum* 'Aureum' makes a splendid small specimen tree, with the bonus of leaves that turn reddish crimson in autumn before falling.

The heights and spreads given for plants in this chapter are those twenty years after being planted in good soil. Where plants continue to grow after this period ultimate heights are also given.

Left: **Genista cinerea** *creates a dazzling dense splash of colour. Here, this deciduous shrub is seen framed by stone walls and a gravel path, which help to soften the impact of the intense yellow flowers and allow it to blend in with its surroundings.*

Acer japonicum 'Aureum'

This beautiful, slow-growing, deciduous bushy tree has bright yellow, seven to eleven-lobed leaves. They are displayed in irregular layers, and in autumn turn rich crimson. It is an ideal tree for a small garden.

Height: 4.5-6m (15-20ft)
Spread: 3.5-4.5m (12-15ft)
Cultivation: Well-drained but moist soil in slight shade suits it best, as the foliage may be scorched in strong sunlight. It does well in chalky soils. No regular pruning is needed, other than initial shaping.
Propagation: It needs to be budded or grafted, and this is best left to expert nurserymen.

Left: **Acer japonicum 'Aureum'** *is a superb small maple for a lawn or in a mixed border. During autumn, the bright yellow leaves become rich crimson. Select a position sheltered from cold winds.*

Below: **Berberis darwinii** *A widely-grown shrub, glowing with flowers in spring. It often forms a sprawling bush, with long shoots intermingled with neighbouring shrubs. When grown as a hedge, it requires regular pruning after flowering to keep it in shape.*

Berberis darwinii

Darwin's Berberis (UK and USA)

This beautiful hardy evergreen shrub bears drooping bunches of flowers amid stalkless glossy, dark-green spiny leaves. From mid to late spring, it bears deep orange-yellow flowers. During late summer and early autumn there is a profusion of purplish-blue oval berries along the shoots.

Height: 1.7-3m (6-10ft)
Spread: 1.8-3m (6-10ft)
Cultivation: It succeeds in any good soil and in full light or slight shade, but position it away from drying winds. The only pruning required is to cut back straggly shoots after flowering.
Propagation: Although it can be increased from seed sown in April in the open soil, the plants do not always produce replicas of the parent. Therefore, take 7.5-10cm (3-4in) long cuttings with heels during late summer, inserting them into pots of equal parts of peat and sharp sand and place them in a

Acer japonicum 'Aureum' looks superb in a border, with underplantings of the spring-flowering *Crocus vernus* or variegated hostas. It also does well as a specimen in a lawn, or in a large tub on a patio.

Berberis darwinii although tall and spreading, can be set near the edge of a path if shoots are cut back after flowering. This allows both the spring flowers and the late summer berries to be admired.

cold frame. Set the rooted plants out into a nursery bed the following spring. Alternatively, pot up the rooted plants into large pots. This makes them easier to transplant into their permanent positions at a later date. This is a shrub frequently grown to form a spring-flowering hedge. If used as such, prune the plants by a quarter immediately after planting them, to encourage bushy growth.

Calceolaria integrifolia

(Calceolaria rugosa)

This half-hardy, upright, bushy, semi-shrubby evergreen perennial has bright yellow, pouch-like flowers, 12-25mm (½-1in) long, from mid to late summer. It grows outside only in warm areas, and even then requires the protection of a south or west-facing wall. The finely-wrinkled, matt, mid-green leaves are lance-shaped.
Height: 1.2m (4ft)
Spread: 1.2-1.5m (4-5ft)
Cultivation: Light, well-drained fertile soil — neutral to acid — is best, and a position in full sun or partial shade. Usually the plants are discarded after flowering, but occasionally in warm and frost-free areas they may become perennial. Plants that do survive winter may still be cut back by cold weather, and are therefore best pruned in late spring to encourage new growth to develop.
Propagation: The plant is best increased from 7.5cm (3in) long heel cuttings in late summer, inserted into pots of equal parts peat and sharp sand. Keep these at 15°C (59°F) and when the cuttings have rooted, pot them up into peat-based compost. Plant them out into the garden in autumn.

Right: **Calceolaria integrifolia**
The vivid-yellow, pouch-like flowers of this half-hardy perennial are eye-catching. But grow it outside only in warm areas and with the protection of a south or west-facing wall.

Calceolaria integrifolia, with its pouch-shaped flowers, gains its generic name because the flower parts resemble a shoe. In Latin, the word for shoemaker is *calceolarius*.

Catalpa bignonioides 'Aurea'

Golden Indian Bean Tree (UK)

Few trees with yellow foliage have more eye-catching leaves than this neatly-shaped, hardy deciduous tree for a small garden. The heart-shaped, rich yellow leaves, 10-25cm (4-10in) long and 7.5-20cm (3-8in) wide, remain attractive throughout summer. During mid-summer there are purple and yellow foxglove-like flowers.

Height: 6-7.5m (20-25ft)
Spread: 6-7.5m (20-25ft)
Cultivation: Catalpas appreciate any good garden soil and a position in full sun, slightly sheltered from cold winds. No regular pruning is needed, other than occasionally shaping the tree in early spring.

Propagation: During late summer, take 7.5-10cm (3-4in) long heel cuttings, inserting them into pots containing equal parts peat and sharp sand, and keeping them at 18°C (64°F). When the cuttings are rooted, pot them up into small pots and overwinter in a cold frame. In spring, set them out in a nursery bed for three or four years before transplanting to their final positions.

Below: **Chamaecyparis lawsoniana 'Lutea'**
A beautiful golden conifer, raised in North America more than one hundred years ago. It requires a sunny position for the golden-yellow foliage to keep its colour throughout the year.

Right: **Catalpa bignonioides 'Aurea'**
The beautiful, soft-textured, woolly, heart-shaped leaves of this deciduous tree retain their golden-yellow colour throughout summer. They are a perfect match for the purple and yellow flowers.

Chamaecyparis lawsoniana 'Lutea'

This golden-yellow-foliaged form of the evergreen conifer, Lawson's Cypress, is a well-tried favourite for small gardens. It has an upward, relatively narrow stance, with a drooping, spire-like top and flattened, somewhat feathery sprays of slightly-drooping foliage.

Height: 9m (30ft)
Spread: 1.5-1.8m (5-6ft)
Cultivation: Well-drained garden soil and an open but sheltered position suit it best. In shady positions it tends to become green. No pruning is required, except during early years, when you should cut out second-leader shoots during spring.

Propagation: Seeds can be sown in spring, but the seedlings will not necessarily reflect the nature of the parent. Named forms are best raised in spring from heel cuttings 10cm (4in) long, inserted into pots containing equal parts of peat and sharp sand and kept at 16°C (61°F). When the cuttings are

Catalpa bignonioides 'Aurea' is excellent for a small garden. It can be grown in a lawn, or mixed with other plants in a border. However, do not place high plants in front of it, or they spoil its shape.

Chamaecyparis lawsoniana 'Lutea' can be grown as a specimen in a grouping with other conifers, or in a mixed border where its size and colour will break up visually long vistas.

Propagation: Seeds can be sown when ripe in late summer, but they take up to two years to germinate. Often the plant has low-growing roots and these can be layered in late summer and early autumn. They take about two years to produce roots. Another method is to take 7.5-10cm (3-4in) long half-ripe heel cuttings in mid to late summer. Insert them in equal parts peat and sharp sand and place in a propagation frame at 16°C (61°F). When they are rooted, place them in a cold frame.

Below: **Cornus mas**
The clusters of small golden-yellow flowers are a delight in late winter and early spring. The fruits of this European native have been used for sweetmeats and tarts. The Turks used the flowers to control diarrhoea, as a preventative for cholera, and for flavouring sherbet. The hard wood has been used to make forks, ladder-spokes and butchers' skewers.

rooted, pot them up into small pots and plant them out into a nursery bed during the following year for three or four seasons before setting them in their final site.

Cornus mas

Cornelian Cherry (UK)
Cornelian Cherry · Sorbet (USA)

This is a distinctive late winter and early spring flowering deciduous shrub. It is somewhat twiggy and bushy, with 1.2-2.5cm (½-1in) long clusters of golden-yellow flowers. These are borne along naked branches and are sometimes followed by bright red, edible cherry-like fruits. The dark green leaves turn reddish-purple in autumn. The form 'Aurea' has leaves suffused yellow.
Height: 2.4-3.5m (8-12ft)
Spread: 1.8-3m (6-10ft)
Cultivation: Any good garden soil, including clay, suits it. Position it in full sun, if possible, although it will tolerate light shade. No regular pruning is needed, other than an initial shaping when young.

Cornus mas is a delight in winter, but unfortunately its branches often spread to soil-level, making it impossible to set plants beneath it. However, it is possible to train on a long main stem.

Cupressus macrocarpa 'Goldcrest'

This beautiful, hardy, densely-foliaged, medium-sized evergreen conifer has rich yellow, feathery, scale-like foliage. It has a narrow, columnar outline which broadens slightly with age. It is excellent for coastal areas and can also be planted to form a hedge. In ten years, it should have grown 4m (13ft) high and 1m (3½ft) wide.
Height: 9-18m (30-60ft)
Spread: 1.5-1.8m (5-6ft)
Cultivation: Any well-drained garden soil and a sunny, open

Left: **Cupressus macrocarpa 'Goldcrest'**
This is a superbly-coloured form of the Monterey Cypress. It forms a striking focal point in a lawn or border, and also looks good in a colour-contrasting collection of conifers, especially blue ones.

Cupressus macrocarpa 'Goldcrest' blends well in groupings with blue-foliaged conifers such as *Picea pungens* 'Koster' and silver-barked trees like birches. In a large garden, try a grouping of cupressus and silver birches, underplanted with daffodils.

position suit this lovely conifer. No regular pruning is needed, other than removing double leader shoots in spring.

Propagation: Seeds can be sown in spring, but the seedlings will not resemble the parent. Instead, take 7.5-10cm (3-4in) long heel cuttings during autumn, inserting them into pots of equal parts peat and sharp sand and placing them in a cold frame. When the cuttings are rooted, pot them up into small pots and plunge these in a nursery bed. Set the plants out into their final positions in the garden in autumn when they are well grown and sturdy.

Below: **Cupressus macrocarpa**
The golden form of this magnificent conifer forms an eye-catching hedge that can be used as a backdrop for dark-leaved plants, or as an attractive feature on its own. It looks best when positioned in good sunlight.

Above: **Cytisus scoparius 'Golden Sunlight'**
The rich yellow, pea-shaped flowers are dominant in early summer. The plant often appears bare when flowering is over, and is therefore best positioned in a mixed border where colour can be continued by other plants.

Cytisus scoparius

Common Broom (UK)
Scotch Broom (USA)

This is an upright, free-flowering deciduous shrub with pea-shaped, rich-yellow flowers, 2.5cm (1in) long, borne singly or in pairs during early summer. Although deciduous, its green stems give it an evergreen appearance. There are several superb forms, including 'Andreanus' (yellow and chocolate flowers), 'Burkwoodii' (shades of maroon, purple and red), 'Golden Sunlight' (rich yellow flowers) and 'Sulphureus' (sulphur-yellow flowers).

Height: 1.5-2.5m (5-8ft)
Spread: 1.5-2.1m (5-7ft)
Cultivation: Well-drained, deep, neutral or slightly acid soils are best, and plenty of sun. After flowering, cut off about two-thirds of the previous season's shoots. It is often easier to do this with a pair of garden shears.
Propagation: It can be increased from seeds sown in spring and placed in a cold frame, but it is easier to take 7.5-10cm (3-4in) long heel cuttings during late summer. Insert them into pots containing equal parts of peat and sharp sand and place them in a cold frame. Pot them into pots of peat-based compost when they have rooted, and plant out into the garden in autumn.

Cytisus scoparius is the parent of many forms, including the Moonlight Broom (*Cytisus scoparius* 'Sulphureus'). This is an attractive compact form, with creamy sulphur-yellow flowers, tinged red when in bud, during early summer.

TREES AND SHRUBS

This is one of the most popular of spring-flowering shrubs, its rich yellow flowers appearing with the newly-emerging leaves. Forsythias are named in commemoration of William Forsyth, who was Superintendent of the Royal Gardens at Kensington, London, about 200 years ago.

Forsythia x intermedia

Few spring-flowering plants can match the colour impact of this vigorous, deciduous hardy hybrid shrub. It has golden-yellow, bell-shaped flowers, 2.5-3cm (1-1¼in) wide, in groups of up to six on the previous year's shoots. The leaves are lance-shaped, toothed and dark green. Several superb forms are available, including 'Spectabilis' with large rich yellow flowers, and 'Lynwood' with very large golden-yellow flowers. The form 'Spectabilis' can also be used to form hedges.

Height: 2.4-3m (8-10ft)
Spread: 2.1-2.4m (7-8ft)
Cultivation: Most garden soils are suitable, in sun or partial shade. They are a good choice for town gardens. If you want to grow a hedge of 'Spectabilis', set the plants 45-60cm (1½-2ft) apart in late autumn, cutting the shoots back to soil-level to encourage bushiness from ground-level. Because flowers are borne mainly on shoots which developed during the previous season, cut out a few of the oldest shoots from the base each spring after flowering. At the same time, remove dead wood and twiggy growths from the centre of the shrub. Hedges need a light clipping in spring.
Propagation: Home gardeners can readily increase forsythia in autumn, by taking hardwood cuttings, 25-30cm (10-12in) long, of the current year's growth. Insert them in a nursery bed in the garden; rooting takes about a year. Then plant in their final sites.

Forsythias are, to many people, the epitome of spring and the beginning of the gardener's year. The cheerful yellow flowers add to those of naturalized daffodils to paint a strongly-coloured spring picture.

Height: 60cm-1.2m (2-4ft)
Spread: 1.5-2.1m (5-7ft)
Cultivation: Give genistas a well-drained, slightly acid or neutral soil and a position in full sun. They do not like rich soil as this encourages soft growth, quickly damaged by frost. Because plants are difficult to transplant, use only container-grown ones. No regular pruning is required, other than thinning out congested and dead shoots after flowering. However, a light clipping at this time helps the development of further shoots, as well as maintaining an attractive and manageable mound-like shape.
Propagation: It can be increased from seeds, but the easiest method is to take 7.5-10cm (3-4in) long heel cuttings during late summer, insert them into pots of equal parts peat and sharp sand and place them in a cold frame. Pot the cuttings into peat-based compost when they are rooted, and transplant them into the garden in late autumn.

Below: **Genista hispanica**
This early summer-flowering shrub, native of south-west Europe, grows best on poor, well-drained soils. Rich soils encourage lush growth that is vulnerable to frost damage.

Left: **Forsythia**
As an added dimension, a forsythia can be grown on a stem and planted to blend with a white fence and to act as a focal point in the corner of a garden.

Genista hispanica

Spanish Gorse (UK)
Spanish Broom (USA)

A dense, spiny and hairy deciduous shrub, best suited to warm areas. The deep green, exceptionally narrow leaves are borne on upright stems, and the golden-yellow, pea-shaped, 2.5m (1in) wide flowers appear from early to mid-summer. When it is in full flower, the colour is so intense that the whole shrub appears blessed with a golden glow.

Genista hispanica produces a dense, spreading display of startlingly yellow flowers. Its spreading habit makes it ideal for covering large, warm, dry areas, and its mounded shape is attractive.

Above: **Hamamelis mollis**
The spider-like fragrant, golden-yellow flowers of this small Chinese tree or large shrub have made it a firm favourite in many gardens. The branches have a zigzag spreading habit.

Hamamelis mollis

Chinese Witch Hazel (UK and USA)

Of all winter to early-spring flowering plants, this hardy deciduous small tree or large shrub is perhaps the most memorable. The sweetly-scented, golden-yellow flowers, 2.5-3cm (1-1¼in) wide, are formed of spider-like petals clustered along the base twigs. The broad, roundish, rather pear-shaped mid-green leaves are a delight in autumn, when they turns a beautiful yellow before falling. The form 'Pallida' bears large, sulphur-yellow and sweetly-scented flowers from late winter.

Height: 1.8-2.4m (6-8ft)
Spread: 1.8-2.4m (6-8ft)
Cultivation: Fertile, moisture-retentive, light to medium-textured neutral or slightly acid soil is best. Set the plant in full sun or light shade, and shelter it from cold winds. Little pruning is required, except for the removal in spring of dead or straggly branches.
Propagation: Although it can be increased from seeds, as well as 10cm (4in) long heel cuttings in late summer, the easiest way for home gardeners is to layer low-growing shoots in early autumn. Rooting takes about two years.

Hamamelis mollis has spreading branches, allowing plenty of light to reach plants close to it during winter and spring. The winter-flowering *Rhododendron mucronulatum* with funnel-shaped, rose-purple flowers makes an attractive contrast.

Hypericum 'Hidcote'

(Hypericum patulum 'Hidcote')

This is a hardy, semi-evergreen compact shrub, with wide, lance-shaped deep green leaves. During summer it displays 4-5cm (1½-2in) wide, saucer-shaped, golden-yellow flowers near the ends of the shoots. It is a reliable shrub, and justifiably one of the most popular. Many other hypericums can be grown in our gardens, including the well-known Rose of Sharon (*Hypericum calycinum*), also known as Aaron's Beard. With its golden-yellow flowers, up to 7.5cm (3in) wide, and its tough, durable nature it is ideal for covering sunny, well-drained banks. Steep slopes in gardens become awash with colour from its flowers from early summer to early autumn. It forms a dense mass of ground-covering, bright-green leaves by sending out spreading roots.

Height: 90cm-1.8m (3-6ft)
Spread: 1.5-2.1m (5-7ft)
Cultivation: Hypericum prefers a fertile, well-drained but moisture-retentive soil and a sunny or slightly shaded position. It will tolerate slightly alkaline soils. Little pruning is required, although occasionally it may be damaged by frosts. If this happens, cut back the shoots to their bases in spring, and at the same time remove weak or diseased shoots.
Propagation: Softwood cuttings can be taken in summer, but it is often easier to take 10-13cm (4-5in) long cuttings in late summer, insert them into pots containing equal parts of peat and sharp sand and place them in a cold frame. The following year, the cuttings can be set out in a nursery bed and transplanted to their permanent sites when well-grown and sturdy.

Left: **Hypericum 'Hidcote'**
This is an exceptionally reliable shrub for the garden, with large saucer-shaped, golden-yellow flowers through most of the summer. The flowers appear slightly above the foliage.

Hypericum 'Hidcote' is useful for filling large areas in shrub borders with bright colour. It can also be positioned at the junction of paths, where it can be used as a focal point; however, it eventually needs plenty of space, if it is not to encroach on the path.

Juniperus chinensis 'Aurea'

Young's Golden Juniper · Golden Chinese Juniper (UK)

A distinctive slow-growing, tall, slender evergreen conifer with golden foliage, this shrub is ideal for small town gardens, reaching only 1.5m (5ft) high and 80cm (32in) wide in ten years. It has two types of foliage: needle-like young leaves, and scale-like adult ones.
Height: 6m (20ft)
Spread: 1m (3½ft)
Cultivation: Ordinary well-drained soil and a position in full sun are best. No regular pruning is needed.
Propagation: Seeds can be sown in late summer and autumn, but the plants do not come true from named forms. Therefore, in late summer take 5-10cm (2-4in) long heel cuttings, inserting them into pots containing equal parts of peat and sharp sand and place them in a cold frame. When rooted, pot up the cuttings singly into small pots and plunge these into a nursery bed. This helps to keep the compost moist and cool. Plant them out in the garden in late autumn while the soil is still warm, to encourage rooting.

Left: **Juniperus chinensis 'Aurea'**
This golden form of the Chinese Juniper was raised at Young's Nursery in Surrey, England, thereby gaining one of its common names. It bears both juvenile and adult foliage simultaneously, producing a two-tone effect.

Kerria japonica

Jew's Mallow (UK)
Japanese Rose (USA)

This is a beautiful spring and early-summer flowering deciduous shrub with arching shoots. The long apple-green stems bear bright green, toothed, lance-shaped leaves. The 4cm (1½in) wide single flowers are borne on the ends of the previous season's stems. It is the form 'Pleniflora' that is chiefly grown, with double, 5cm (2in) wide, bright orange-yellow flowers. A variegated form is also available, with creamy-white edges to the leaves.
Height: 1.2-1.8m (4-6ft)
Spread: 1.5-1.8m (5-6ft)
Cultivation: Ordinary garden soil is

Right: **Juniperus chinensis**
A golden form of this spectacular evergreen forms an exciting focal point in a sea of heathers and with a background of dark-leaved conifers. The large yellow conifer at the left of the juniperus is Chamaecyparis lawsoniana 'Winston Churchill'.

suitable. As soon as flowering has finished, cut back the flowered shoots of 'Pleniflora' to encourage the development of strong shoots.
Propagation: It can be increased from 10cm (4in) long hardwood cuttings in autumn, inserting them into pots containing equal parts of peat and sharp sand. During the following spring, set the rooted cuttings in a nursery bed. An easier way is to dig up rooted stems during autumn or spring.

Below: **Kerria japonica 'Pleniflora'**
The deeply-toothed, bright green leaves are a perfect foil for the double orange-yellow flowers. Kerrias were introduced into the British Isles in 1804 by William Kerr the British plant-hunter.

Juniperus chinensis 'Aurea' is superb in a heather garden, contrasting with heathers and other conifers, especially those with a spreading and prostrate growth habit. It can also be positioned against blue-foliaged conifers.

Kerria japonica 'Pleniflora' looks superb planted
against a south or west-facing wall. In such a
position, it is essential to encourage spring growths
from soil level. Small blue-flowered bulbs, such as
crocuses, do well at its base.

TREES AND SHRUBS

Left: **Laburnum anagyroides**
When trained over a pergola, its pendulous flowers form a stunning canopy in late spring. But it is a tree that is poisonous, and should not be planted near a fish pool, or in gardens with inquisitive children.

Potentilla 'Elizabeth'

Cinquefoil (UK and USA)

Few shrubs display their flowers for such a long period as this hardy deciduous shrub. The 2.5cm (1in) wide, canary-yellow flowers appear from early summer to

Laburnum anagyroides

(Laburnum vulgare)
Common Laburnum (UK)
Golden Chain (USA)

This small deciduous tree bears golden-yellow, pea-shaped flowers in drooping sprays 15-25cm (6-10in) long, in late spring and early summer. The slightly hairy, dull green leaves are formed of three leaflets. As the tree ages, it tends to spread. For extra yellow colour, choose the form 'Aureum' with soft yellow leaves which slowly become green during the growing season. Occasionally, this laburnum is trained over a pergola to produce a tunnel of glorious colour when in full flower.
Height: 3-5.4m (10-18ft)
Spread: 2.4-3.5m (8-12ft)
Cultivation: Laburnums like a well-drained garden soil in full sun or slight shade. Ensure that the tree is well supported during its early years. The seedpods are poisonous to humans and to fish, so take care to prevent children from investigating them, and do not plant a laburnum tree near a fish pool. No pruning is needed, other than an initial shaping of the tree in summer.
Propagation: Seeds can be sown in autumn and placed in a cold frame. However, named forms do not come true from seed and are therefore grafted on to special rootstocks in the nursery.

Below: **Potentilla x 'Elizabeth'** *This shrubby Cinquefoil is one of the gems of the garden, with bright canary-yellow flowers from early summer to autumn. It is an extremely reliable shrub that needs little attention.*

Laburnums form a happy and colourful combination with lilacs, especially those with blue flowers. Even when planted several yards apart, the two trees create a beautiful picture.

autumn and are borne singly or in twos and threes. They stand slightly above the mid-green, deeply-cut leaves. There are several other superb forms, including 'Farreri' (bright yellow) and 'Katherine Dykes' (primrose-yellow).

Height: 90cm-1.2m (3-4ft)
Spread: 1.2-1.5m (4-5ft)
Cultivation: Any good well-drained garden soil suits it, and a position in full sun. No regular pruning is needed, other than cutting out dead and old stems during spring.
Propagation: Take 5-7.5cm (2-3in) long cuttings in spring, set them in pots containing equal parts of peat and sharp sand and place them in a cold frame. Alternatively, lift and divide large clumps in spring.

Below: **Laburnum anagyroides** *These bright-flowered trees are occasionally used as street trees. However, remember that all parts of the tree are poisonous, especially the seeds.*

Shrubby potentillas can be grown as informal hedges. Set the plants 75-90cm (2½-3ft) apart, but allow for their spread when positioning them alongside a path or boundary.

TREES AND SHRUBS

Robinia pseudoacacia 'Frisia'

Black Locust · False Acacia (UK)
Black Locust · Common Locust ·
Yellow Locust (USA)

This is a beautiful, small to medium-sized form of the Common Acacia. It has deciduous golden-yellow leaves. From spring to autumn it reveals pinnate leaves formed of up to eleven pairs of leaflets, first golden-yellow, then pale greenish-yellow in mid to late summer.

Height: 6-7m (20-26ft)
Spread: 3-3.5m (10-12ft)
Cultivation: Robinia thrives in any well-drained soil and a sunny position. Avoid cold and exposed areas. No regular pruning is required, but if any shaping is needed, it is best carried out during mid-summer when there is less chance of the tree bleeding.
Propagation: It is best to buy plants from a reputable nurseryman, as the propagation of the tree involves grafting the species on to stocks of *Robinia pseudoacacia* in spring.

Robinia pseudoacacia 'Frisia' is useful for providing colour contrasts. The 1.8-2.4m (6-8ft) high *Cotinus coggygria* 'Royal Purple', with dark plum-coloured foliage, makes an excellent companion.

Far left: **Robinia pseudoacacia 'Frisia'**
The golden-yellow leaves formed of many leaflets create a beautiful and graceful tree, even for small gardens. It provides continuing interest from spring to autumn.

Left: **Senecio 'Sunshine'**
This New Zealand plant, with its daisy-like yellow flowers in early summer, is a delight in any garden. It is also attractive during winter, when the silvery-grey leaves are covered with frost.

Right: **Taxus baccata 'Fastigiata Aurea'**
A beautiful yew with golden foliage, especially attractive when planted in full sun. Initially, it suits rock gardens, but eventually becomes too large for a restricted site.

Senecio 'Sunshine'

A widely-grown evergreen shrub, known for many years as *Senecio greyi* or *S. laxifolius*. It is a spreading, mound-forming — sometimes straggly — shrub, with silver-grey leaves that turn green with age. During early summer, it produces yellow, daisy-like flowers 2.5cm (1in) across. During winter, the leaves look handsome when they are covered by frost or a light dusting of snow. Unfortunately, heavy snow falls can flatten and destroy the shrub's attractive mounded form.
Height: 1-1.2m (3-4½ft)
Spread: 1.2-1.5m (4-5ft)
Cultivation: Ordinary well-drained garden soil in full sun is ideal. It does well in coastal areas. Occasionally, it is damaged by severe frosts and heavy snow falls; if this happens, cut out the dead shoots in spring. Straggly plants should also be cut back in spring.
Propagation: During late summer, take 7.5-10cm (3-4in) long half-ripe cuttings. Insert them into pots of equal parts peat and sharp sand and place them in a cold frame. When they are rooted, transplant them to the garden.

Taxus baccata 'Fastigiata Aurea'

Golden Irish Yew (UK)

This is a neat, upright, golden evergreen conifer, a form of the Irish Yew. It has a solid appearance, with tight foliage. It is slow-growing, reaching 2m (6½ft) high and about 60cm (2ft) wide after ten years.
Height: 4.5m (15ft)
Spread: 75-90cm (2½-3ft)
Cultivation: Well-drained soil, acid or alkaline, suits it. A position in full sun is essential to encourage good foliage colour. No regular pruning is needed.
Propagation: It has to be increased by 7.5-10cm (3-4in) long heel cuttings in late summer and early autumn. Insert them into pots of equal parts peat and sharp sand and place them in a cold frame. Pot them on into pots of peat compost and plant them out in the garden when well-grown.

Senecio 'Sunshine' is best positioned near the front of a border or next to a path. Its mounded form becomes completely covered with flowers. It also looks good at a junction of two paths.

Taxus baccata, the Common Yew, is the parent of several golden-leaved forms, including 'Aurea' (slow-growing, compact, with young golden-yellow foliage) and 'Dovastonii Aurea' (leaves edged yellow).

Left: **Taxus baccata 'Semperaurea'**
A beautiful golden form of the English Yew. It develops slowly into a medium-sized shrub, with the yellow colour at its most intense during spring.

Taxus baccata 'Semperaurea'

This is a slow-growing, densely-packed, golden-foliaged version of the Yew. The new foliage is golden on first opening in spring, and slowly becomes rusty-yellow for the rest of the year. It grows to about 1m (3½ft) high in ten years.
Height: 3m (10ft)
Spread: 1.5-2.1m (5-7ft)
Cultivation: Most garden soils, in full sun or shade will do. Yews are very adaptable plants, able to thrive in peat-rich, acid soils and chalky soils alike. No regular pruning is needed, but it can be clipped to a preferred shape.
Propagation: Take 7.5-10cm (3-4in) long heel cuttings in late summer and early autumn. Insert them into pots containing equal parts of peat and sharp sand, and place them in a cold frame. Pot them on and plant out when they are well-grown and sturdy.

Ulex europaeus

Gorse · Whin · Furze (UK and USA)

A hardy, sharply-spined, densely-branched evergreen shrub with scale-like leaves that soon fall. From spring to early summer it displays 1.8-2.5cm (¾-1in) long, pea-shaped, golden-yellow flowers. The flowers often appear intermittently until late winter. It is the double-flowered form 'Plenus', with compact hummocks of flowers, that is most often seen in gardens.
Height: 1.5-2.1m (5-7ft)
Spread: 1.5-2.1m (5-7ft)
Cultivation: Gorse needs a light, well-drained poor soil and a position in full sun. Little pruning is needed, but leggy shrubs can be cut back in spring to encourage

---

Taxus baccata 'Fastigiata Aurea' can be used to form an attractive hedge. Set the plants 38cm (15in) apart, sprinkling bonemeal in the planting holes to encourage rapid root development. Firm planting is essential to ensure quick establishment.

new growths from the base.
Propagation: Sow seeds in spring, placing them in a cold frame. Alternatively, take 7.5cm (3in) long cuttings in late summer and insert them into pots containing equal parts of peat and sharp sand. Place these in a cold frame and pot up the plants into pots of peat compost when rooted, transplanting them into the garden in late autumn.

Below: **Ulex europaeus**
This densely-spined, evergreen shrub is hardy in even the most severe weather. It forms an attractive windbreak or boundary. Bright golden-yellow, pea-shaped flowers appear during spring and early summer.

Further plants to consider

Berberis thunbergii 'Aurea'

Height: 90cm-1.5m (3-5ft)   Spread: 75cm-1.2m (2½-4ft)
A distinctive deciduous berberis, with yellow leaves turning pale green by late autumn.

Coronilla glauca

Height: 1.5-1.8m (5-6ft)   Spread: 1.2-1.5m (4-5ft)
A rounded, dense, bushy evergreen shrub, with glaucous leaves and rich yellow scented flowers from early to mid-summer.

Gleditsia triacanthos 'Sunburst'

Height: 5.4-7.5m (18-25ft)   Spread: 3-4.5m (10-15ft)
A deciduous tree with bright golden-yellow young foliage, each leaf formed of up to thirty-two narrow lance-shaped leaflets.

Halimium ocymoides

Height: 60-90cm (2-3ft)   Spread: 90cm-1.2m (3-4ft)
A small, hardy, compact, evergreen shrub, ideal for a large rock garden. During mid-summer, it boasts 2.5cm (1in) wide bright yellow flowers with chocolate blotches at the base of the petals.

Mahonia aquifolium

Oregon Grape

Height: 90cm-1.5m (3-5ft)   Spread: 1.5-1.8m (5-6ft)
A well-known and widely-grown mahonia, with dark green, leathery leaves. During early spring, it bears terminal clusters of fragrant rich yellow flowers, followed by bunches of blue-black berries.

Mahonia x 'Charity'

Height: 1.8-2.4m (6-8ft)   Spread: 1.5-2.1m (5-7ft)
A hardy evergreen with fragrant, rich yellow flowers borne at the tips of the shoots during winter and into early spring.

Rhododendron luteum

Height: 1.8-2.4m (6-8ft)   Spread: 1.5-2.1m (5-7ft)
A well-known deciduous shrub with fragrant, rich yellow flowers during early summer. It is an ideal plant for the wild garden, and does well in slight shade.

Rosa xanthina 'Canary Bird'

Height: 1.5-1.8m (5-6ft)   Spread: 1.2-1.8m (4-6ft)
A deciduous shrub rose, with beautiful clusters of semi-double bright yellow flowers during early to mid-summer.

Sambucus racemosa 'Plumosa Aurea'

Golden Cut-leaved Elder (UK)

Height: 2.1-2.4m (7-8ft)   Spread: 1.8-2.1m (6-7ft)
An eye-catching deciduous shrub with finely-cut golden leaves. During spring, it displays white flowers. It is a plant which looks good when set in front of a dark-leaved hedge, such as yew.

Ulex europaeus is native to western Europe, including the British Isles, and north-west Africa. At one time, it was an important feature in the British landscape, where it formed 'furze-brakes' which were given local place names.

INDEX

COMMON NAMES

Names set in *italic* type are those used in North America.

INDEX

LATIN NAMES

CREDITS

Photographers
The majority of the photographs in this book have been taken by Eric Crichton © Salamander Books Ltd.

Copyright in the following photographs belongs to the suppliers:
Pat Brindley: 28 (Top left)
Eric Crichton: 22 (Right), 29 (Left), 33 (Top right), 33 (Bottom), 37, 74 (Top), 74 (Bottom), 82/83, 88/89, 91
Peter McHoy: 22
David Squire: Front Cover, 6, 7, 10/11, 11, 12, 13, 14/15, 17 (Bottom right), 22 (Left), 27 (Right), 28 (Bottom right), 31 (Right), 32 (Bottom left), 38/39, 56/57, 63, 64/65, 66, 66/67, 67, 68, 69 (Top left), 69 (Bottom right), 70 (Top right), 72/73, 78/79 (Bottom), 80 (Bottom), 82, 85, 87, Back Cover
Michael Warren: 78

Artists
Copyright of the artwork illustrations on the pages following the artists' names is the property of Salamander Books Ltd.
Nicki Kemball: 6/7, 12/13
Steve Linds (Linden Artists): 8, 8/9, 9, 10, 11
Clive Spong (Linden Artists): Front and Back Covers

Editorial Assistance
Proofreading and indexing by Joanna Chapman

PRINTED IN BELGIUM BY

INTERNATIONAL BOOK PRODUCTION